CHILDREN'S WORLD ATLAS

PhP

PETER HADDOCK PUBLISHING

CONTENTS

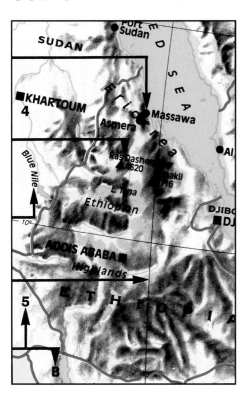

Printed in Europe for
Peter Haddock Publishing, United Kingdom

© Geddes & Grosset, New Lanark, Scotland

Cartography designed and produced by
European Map Graphics Ltd, Pangbourne, England

Picture research by Wade Cooper Associates

ISBN 0 7105 0689 9

3

USING THE ATLAS

MAPS AND ATLASES

A map is a drawing or a plan that shows us the shape, size, main rivers and main towns of a continent, a country, or part of a country. The maps in this atlas will show you all the countries in the world. Some of these you may know quite well, but others may be quite unknown to you.

As well as the maps, on each page there are photographs and text that will help to give you a better picture of what life is like in countries that are not familiar to you. On pages 6 and 7 is a map that shows all the countries of the world, and the pages that follow look at each of the continents in turn.

The maps of a continent can show only a little information about the areas shown, but the maps of countries and regions give more detailed information. It is, however, important to remember that every map can show only a selection of the features that appear in that particular area.

MAP SYMBOLS

Maps are made up of different kinds of symbols. **Area symbols**, by showing an area in one colour, help us to see the shape and size of a country on a map of a continent, or a natural feature such as a lake or sea. Coloured area symbols are also used to show the height of land above sea level. **Line symbols** show features such as roads, railways, rivers, and boundaries. **Point symbols** show us features such as mountain peaks (heights in metres) and towns. Listed below are symbols used on the maps in this atlas.

Height of land in metres
over 5000
4000–5000
3000–4000
2000–3000
1000–2000
500–1000
200–500
0–200
below sea level

▲ 2663   Mountain peak (in metres)
Lake
River
International boundary
State or regional boundary
■   Capital city
●   Other city or town

Abbreviations: sometimes there is not enough space on a map to name a feature in full. Below are abbreviations commonly used in this altas.
Arch.   Archipelago
C.   Cape
Hd.   Head
I.   Island, Isle
Is.   Islands
L.   Lake, Loch
Mt.   Mont, Mount
Mts.   Mountains
Ra.   Range
Str.   Strait
Abbreviations used for country names are listed on the world map or on individual continent maps.

Scale: the scale bar can be used to measure distances on a map. It also tells you by how much the region shown has been reduced.

International boundary: the international boundary tells you where one country meets another one. The boundary often follows the line of a physical feature, such as a river.

Capital city: a capital city is shown on the map by a solid black square symbol. This distinguishes it from other towns and cities on the map.

Map colour: colour is used on maps to show various things. Each country is given a different colour from its neighbour on this map.

Latitude and longitude: lines of latitude and longitude help you to tell how far north or south of the Equator or how far east or west of Greenwich, London, a place is located.

Cities: cities and towns that are not capitals are shown by a solid black circle. The style of lettering of their names is different from that of capital cities.

Mountains: the high peaks in mountain ranges are shown by a small black triangle. The name of a mountain and its height in metres are beside the triangle.

Rivers: rivers are shown on the map by a fine blue line. The name of the river will be found printed along this line.

Map colour: colour is used on this map to show the height of land above sea level.

Grid: places on a map can be found easily by using the grid letters and numbers at the edges of the map. These are needed when using the index.

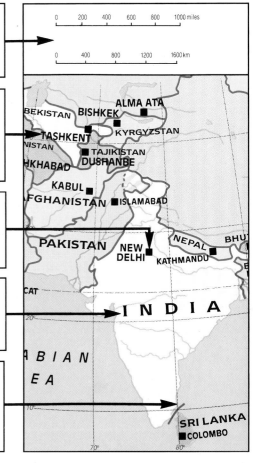

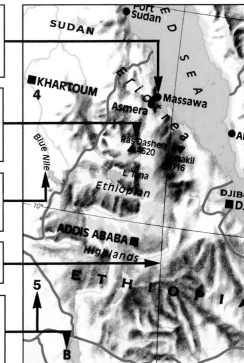

FINDING PLACES

There are two ways to find a place or a feature on the maps in this atlas. On pages 2 and 3 is a list of all the page titles and page numbers that appear on the maps. In order to find a continent, a region or a group of countries it is easy to read the page title and number from this list.

On page 64 a list of names appears. This is the Index, and it will tell you where to find places such as towns, mountains or rivers that are on the maps. The names are arranged in alphabetical order and are all listed in a similar way. For example, the entry for the city of St Petersburg reads:

St Petersburg 30 E4

The entry tells you on which page St Petersburg, formerly Leningrad, a major city in the Russian Federation, appears and the grid square in which it lies on the map. The letters for the grid square appear along the top and bottom of each map, and the numbers are found up both sides.

MAP SCALES

It is impossible to show an area at its true size on a map. All maps in this atlas are therefore drawn at a reduced scale. In order to fit the area we want to show on one page many different scales are used. The maps opposite show how the amount of information given and the area covered on each map are affected by the scale of the map.

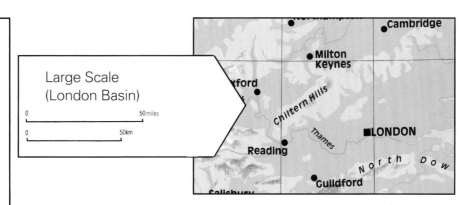

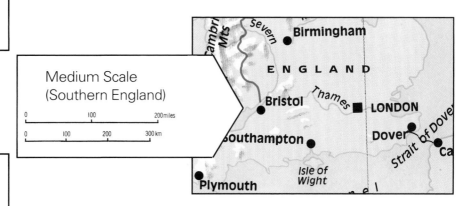

THINGS TO DO

Look carefully at the maps on pages 6 to 63 in this atlas.
Find the map of the country in which you live.
Can you find the capital city of your country?
Look at the map of Africa.
Can you find the longest river in the world?
Look at the map of Central Europe.
Can you find the newly created countries of Slovakia and Latvia?
The highest mountain in the world is Mount Everest.
Can you find it on the map of South Asia and the Middle East?
There are 50 states in the United States of America. Only 49 are shown on page 45.
Which state is missing from this page?

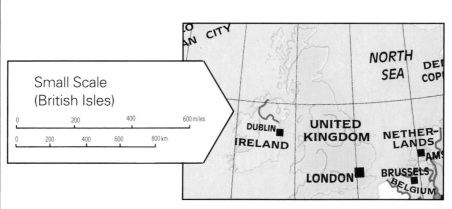

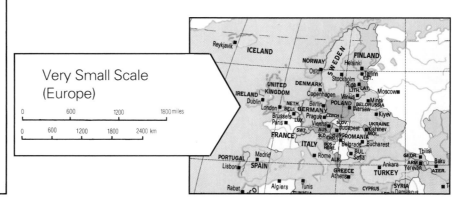

THE WORLD

The world's total surface area is just over 500,000,000 square kilometres. Water makes up two-thirds of this total. The largest areas of water are called oceans. The four oceans of the world are the Pacific, the Atlantic, the Indian and the Arctic Oceans. The Pacific Ocean, which stretches from the east coast of Asia to the west coast of the Americas, is the largest. Smaller areas of water are known as seas. These may be parts of oceans or connected to them by narrow straits. The Mediterranean Sea, which is connected to the Atlantic Ocean by the Strait of Gibraltar, is a good example.

The largest landmasses are called continents. These are Asia, Africa, North America, South America, Oceania, Europe and Antarctica. The largest is Asia and the smallest is Oceania. All the continents, except Antarctica, are made up of different countries. The largest country in the world is the Russian Federation which stretches across Europe and Asia. The smallest country, Vatican City, is 50 million times smaller and is located within Rome, the capital city of Italy.

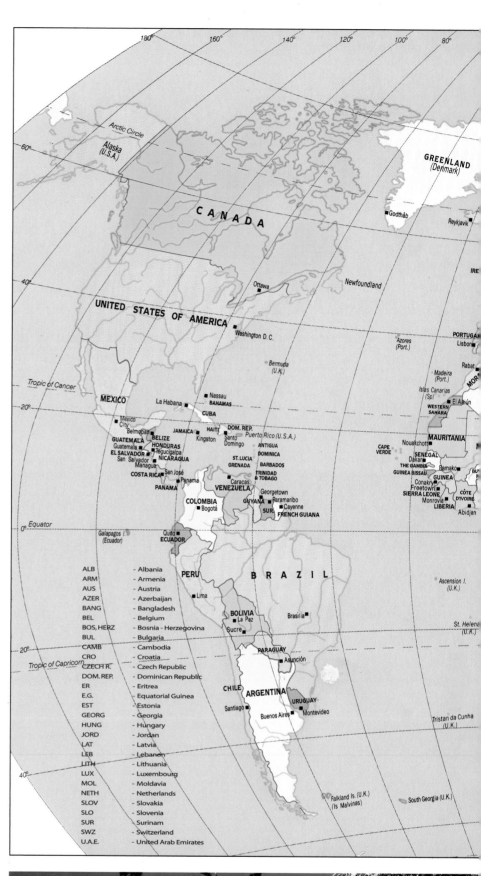

ALB	- Albania
ARM	- Armenia
AUS	- Austria
AZER	- Azerbaijan
BANG	- Bangladesh
BEL	- Belgium
BOS, HERZ	- Bosnia - Herzegovina
BUL	- Bulgaria
CAMB	- Cambodia
CRO	- Croatia
CZECH R.	- Czech Republic
DOM. REP.	- Dominican Republic
ER	- Eritrea
E.G.	- Equatorial Guinea
EST	- Estonia
GEORG	- Georgia
HUNG	- Hungary
JORD	- Jordan
LAT	- Latvia
LEB	- Lebanon
LITH	- Lithuania
LUX	- Luxembourg
MOL	- Moldavia
NETH	- Netherlands
SLOV	- Slovakia
SLO	- Slovenia
SUR	- Surinam
SWZ	- Switzerland
U.A.E.	- United Arab Emirates

Flags of nations have been used throughout history as important symbols to identify countries; often a design reflects how the inhabitants of a nation perceive themselves and their country.

The headquarters of the United Nations are located on Manhattan Island, in the heart of New York City, USA.

The main areas of population within countries are found in cities or towns. These may be large and crowded or may only have a few inhabitants. The largest city in the world is Mexico City, with 10 million inhabitants. It is expected that by the beginning of the 21st century more people will be living in cities than in rural areas.

The Equator, which is an imaginary line around the circumference of the world, extends for 40,075 kilometres. Countries on or near the Equator have very hot climates, but at the Poles, which are the farthest points north and south of the Equator, the climate is extremely cold.

Although the Equator splits the world into two equal parts, it is otherwise very unequal. In general, people in North America, Europe, Japan and Australia are prosperous, have plenty to eat and live in good housing. In contrast, many people living in Africa, South Asia and Central America suffer from malnutrition, poverty and disease. In the prosperous regions, people can expect to live to be 70, whereas in the less developed regions 50 years is the expected life span.

EUROPE: Countries and Capitals

Europe, the second smallest continent, is densely populated and divided into many different countries. Its southern coast fringes the Mediterranean Sea, and it is bounded to the west by the Atlantic Ocean. The northern countries of Norway, Sweden and Finland extend inside the Arctic Circle. Europe's eastern boundary with Asia runs from the Ural Mountains to the Caspian and Black Seas.

There is a great variety of landscapes in Europe. In the south, much of the land is mountainous. The highest peaks are in the Alps. North of these, the land is flatter, and in the far north, Norway and Sweden make up the mountainous Scandinavian Peninsula.

Europe has some extremely fertile land, but the continent is too small and densely populated to be self-supporting in food. It has the greatest concentration of industry of all the continents. The most populated countries are Germany and the European area of Russia. The largest cities are Moscow and Paris, both with over eight million inhabitants, followed by London, St Petersburg (formerly Leningrad) and Berlin.

The flag of the new Europe: twelve gold stars against a blue sky, twelve being the symbol of unity and perfection.

The western countries of Europe are among the richest nations in the world. Fifteen of them form the European Union (EU), once known as the Common Market. The EU was formed as the EC in 1957 with six members, and its main aims were to improve farming, develop industry and raise living standards. The members at present are Belgium, Denmark, France, Germany, Greece, Ireland, Italy, Luxembourg, the Netherlands, Portugal, Spain, Austria, Finland, Sweden and the United Kingdom. The EU has become a political unit where people are able to travel without passports, sell goods in the Union without taxes, and to

CRO	CROATIA
L.	LIECHTENSTEIN
S.M.	SAN MARINO
SWITZ	SWITZERLAND
M	MONACO
MON	MONTENEGRO
V.	VATICAN CITY

The Alps, as one of Europe's main mountain ranges, have always been a natural barrier, but today road and rail tunnels and modern highways provide good communications.

Momentous political changes in Europe led to the Berlin Wall being demolished and the city reunified in the enlarged Germany.

live and work where they wish. Twelve EU countries now have one European currency, the euro.

Since 1990, many changes have taken place in Europe. Borders have been removed and several new republics have emerged. Having been split into the Federal Republic of Germany and the German Democratic Republic for over 40 years, the unification of Germany took place in 1990 after the fall of the Communist government in East Germany. The area of Germany is now 356,755 square kilometres. The capital of the unified country is Berlin, which has replaced Bonn as the seat of government.

In contrast, the former USSR underwent a disintegration of the union in 1991. There are now 15 independent republics, ten of which are all or partly in Europe. A declaration to found a Commonwealth of Independent States was signed by 11 of the republics, but Georgia, Latvia, Lithuania and Estonia opted to remain outside it.

More recently, Yugoslavia has seen the disintegration of its republics. One by one they have broken away to become independent countries: Slovenia, Croatia, Bosnia and Herzegovinia, Macedonia, and finally Serbia and Montenegro which have become a union of two semi-independent states.

THE BRITISH ISLES

The British Isles are situated off the northwest coast of mainland Europe. They are bounded to the west by the Atlantic Ocean, to the north and east by the North Sea, and in the south the English Channel separates them from the rest of Europe. The two main islands of Great Britain and Ireland make up the British Isles. There are also many groups of small islands off the western and northern coasts. The British Isles consist of two separate nations— the United Kingdom and the Republic of Ireland. The United Kingdom is made up of the countries of England, Wales and Scotland on the island of Great Britain, and Northern Ireland in the northeast of the island of Ireland. The Republic of Ireland covers the rest of Ireland.

Through the centuries, the British Isles have been invaded many times. The Romans established a province known as Britannia, which lasted until the 5th century. This covered the area south of Hadrian's Wall, built in AD122, which stretched across northern Britain for 130 kilometres. In the 5th and 6th centuries an Irish tribe known as the Scots invaded Northern Britain. By the 8th century, the Anglo-Saxons had invaded and formed several kingdoms in England. They were followed by the Viking invasions along the east coast. In 1066 the Normans, led by William the Conqueror, invaded and, at the famous Battle of Hastings, defeated Harold, King of England. The Normans ruled for 300 years and formed the framework for government in the Middle Ages. Today the United Kingdom is a constitutional monarchy with the queen as head of state. Ireland is a republic with the president as head of state.

In the 18th century, the Industrial Revolution began in Britain. It became a great manufacturing and trading nation,

The changing of the guard at Buckingham Palace, London, is a daily pageant that symbolises Britain's long regal history.

and it was at this time that Britain expanded its Empire to many parts of the world. Much of Africa, Canada, India, Australia and New Zealand became colonies. During the 20th century, many of these colonies gained independence but are still linked to the UK through the Commonwealth of Nations.

Today the principal industries in the UK include iron and steel, motor vehicles, electronics and electrical engineering, textiles and consumer goods. These industries rely heavily on the import of raw materials. The country is self-sufficient in oil from the North Sea.

The extraction of oil and natural gas from beneath the North Sea, which has taken place since the 1970s, is now an important industry.

Scale

0   100   200   300 km   0   100   200 miles

A   B   C   0°   D   Bergen   E   10° F

ATLANTIC   Shetland   OSLO   60°
                                                    Islands
OCEAN   (U.K.)   N O R W A Y   2
                                                                                                    10°

        Orkney
        Islands

  Outer Hebrides

                Inverness   DENMARK
                        Aberdeen
                                                    N O R T H   Esbjerg
        SCOTLAND
   Glasgow   Edinburgh   55°
                                                    S E A

        U N I T E D   Newcastle—
                                     upon-Tyne
   NORTHERN
   IRELAND   Pennines
            Belfast
                K I N G D O M   Bremen
   Isle of
   Man   Leeds   Hull   NETHERLANDS   3
Irish Sea   AMSTERDAM
IRELAND ■ DUBLIN Liverpool   Rotterdam   Rhine
                        Manchester
                                                                                       GERMANY
            Cambrian   Trent   Antwerp
            Mts.   Severn
   Cork   Birmingham   ■ BRUSSELS   ■ Bonn
            WALES   E N G L A N D   BELGIUM
St. George's Channel Cardiff   Bristol   Thames ■ LONDON   LUX.
                                          Dover   Strait of Dover   LUXEMBOURG
            Southampton   Calais
Lands End   Isle of   50°
Isles Of   Plymouth Wight   BERN ■
Scilly   English Channel   SWITZ.
   Channel Is.
   (U.K.)   Brest   Le Havre

ATLANTIC
                                           PARIS   Seine
OCEAN
                   Nantes   FRANCE
        Bay
                        Loire   Lyon   4
        of
                                    Massif
        Biscay   Central
                                                                               45°

        B   5°   C   WEST FROM   EAST FROM   D 5° E   5°
                                GREENWICH   GREENWICH

11

ENGLAND AND WALES

England and Wales are two constituent countries of the United Kingdom. They are bounded to the west by the Irish Sea and by Scotland to the north. The English Channel and the North Sea separate them from mainland Europe.

The landscape of England comprises the mountains of Cumbria in the north, including Scafell Pike (977 metres), the highest peak, and the Pennines running down the middle of the northern half of the country, flat plains in the east, and lowlands broken by low ranges of hills in the south. In the southwest are the bleak moors and rocky sea cliffs of Devon and Cornwall.

The most densely populated parts of England cover the major urban areas of Manchester, Merseyside, South Yorkshire, Birmingham, West Midlands and Greater London. Nearly one quarter of the workforce is involved in manufacturing. Principal industries include iron and steel, motor vehicles, electronics and electrical engineering, textiles and clothing, aircraft, and consumer goods. Industry relies heavily on imported raw materials.

Tourism is an important industry, and many visitors look no farther than London for their stay. London, the capital city of the United Kingdom, is situated on the river Thames. It has a population of almost seven million and is the centre of government, administration, law and culture. It is also one of the world's most important financial centres. In the heart of the city well-known tourist attractions include Westminster Abbey, the Houses of Parliament and Buckingham Palace, as well as museums containing national collections of paintings and of objects relating to the United Kingdom's history.

Wales is a mountainous country with the highest peaks in the northwest. Snowdon, at 1085

The 13th-century Conway Castle in North Wales was built as a garrison for the occupying English troops of King Edward I.

metres, is the highest mountain. The Vale of Glamorgan and the Isle of Anglesey in the north are the main areas of lowland. The uplands are broken by rivers flowing in all directions through deep valleys. There is a strong feeling of nationalism in Wales, and recently the country was given its own Welsh Assembly which is responsible for some aspects of government. Nearly two-thirds of the population live in the south.

The largest cities are Cardiff, Swansea and Newport. Industry in South Wales developed around the coalfields, once among the most important in the world. Coal mining has declined dramatically, and light industry is now more important.

Tourism is one of Wales's chief industries. There are flourishing resorts around the coast, and three areas of the most beautiful scenery are now national parks.

A typical English village street scene, with shops and pubs traditionally built with local materials.

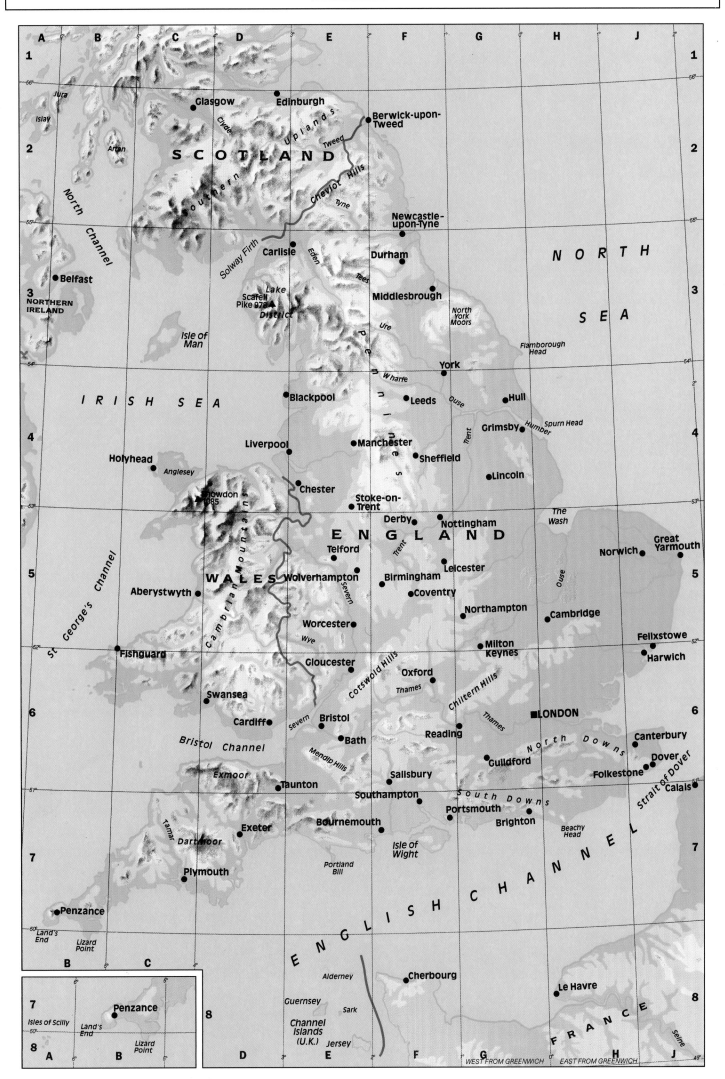

Scale

SCOTLAND

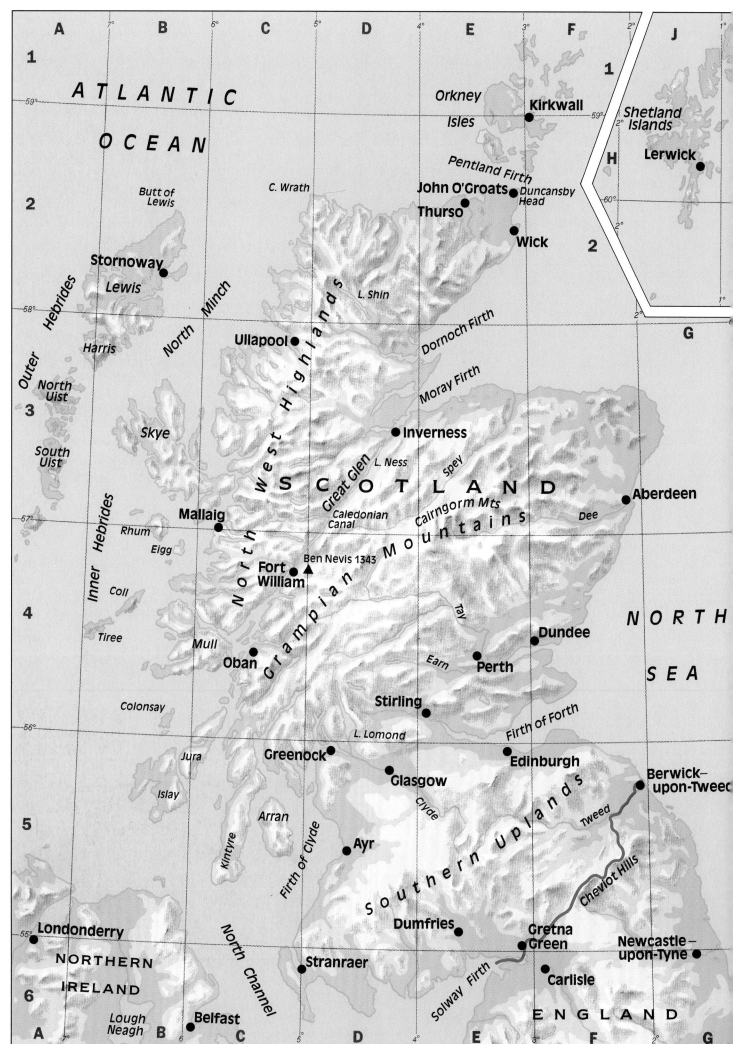

ATLANTIC OCEAN

Orkney Isles
Kirkwall

Shetland Islands
Lerwick

Pentland Firth
John O'Groats
Duncansby Head
Thurso
Wick

Butt of Lewis
C. Wrath

Stornoway
Lewis

North Minch
L. Shin
Dornoch Firth

Outer Hebrides
Harris

Ullapool

North Uist

Moray Firth

Skye

North West Highlands
Inverness

South Uist

Great Glen
L. Ness
Spey

S C O T L A N D

Aberdeen

Inner Hebrides
Rhum
Eigg

Mallaig
Caledonian Canal
Cairngorm Mts
Dee

Coll

Fort William
Ben Nevis 1343
Grampian Mountains

Tiree

Mull
Oban

Tay

N O R T H

Dundee

Earn
Perth

Colonsay

Stirling

S E A

L. Lomond

Jura

Greenock
Firth of Forth

Glasgow
Edinburgh

Clyde
Berwick-upon-Tweed

Islay

Arran

Tweed
Southern Uplands

Ayr
Cheviot Hills

Kintyre
Firth of Clyde

Londonderry

NORTHERN IRELAND

North Channel

Dumfries
Gretna Green
Newcastle-upon-Tyne

Solway Firth
Carlisle

Stranraer

Lough Neagh
Belfast

E N G L A N D

Scotland is the most northern country that is part of the United Kingdom. It consists of the Highlands in the north, the Central Lowlands, and the hilly uplands in the south. There are more mountains in Scotland than in any other region of the United Kingdom. The highest peak in the United Kingdom, Ben Nevis, rises to 1343 metres in the Grampian Mountains.

The Scottish coastline is deeply indented, and there are hundreds of offshore islands. The largest island groups are the Western Isles, which consist of the Outer Hebrides and the Inner Hebrides off the west coast, and the Orkney and Shetland Islands in the far north, which are also known as the Northern Isles.

Another feature of the Scottish landscape is its numerous lochs. Two of the most famous are Loch Lomond, which has attracted tourists for many years, and Loch Ness, which is said to contain the Loch Ness monster.

There is a marked difference in climate between the west and the east coasts of Scotland. In the west it is very wet and mild, but in the east it is drier and colder. On the highest peaks it is often possible to find snow all year round.

The Central Valley of Scotland is the most densely populated area, and it is here that the capital, Edinburgh, and the largest city, Glasgow, are located.

Edinburgh is the second largest financial centre in the United Kingdom after the City of London. It is also an important tourist centre with around two million visitors each year. The city's most dominant landmark is the castle, which stands on a volcanic outcrop known as Castle Rock, at the head of the Royal Mile, a street that leads down through the city to the palace of Holyrood House.

Glasgow in the west is situated on the river Clyde and forms the industrial heartland of the Central Valley. The decline in Scotland's heavy industry after the Second World War left many of the buildings and much of the land in and around Glasgow derelict, but widespread redevelopment and refurbishment have transformed the city. In recent years tourism has become important to Glasgow, which boasts many fine art galleries and museums and is a transport centre for visitors to the Highlands and Islands.

The *Bealach na Ba*, Scots Gaelic for "pass of the cattle", is an ancient route through the mountainous wilderness of the scenic Highlands, now favoured by tourists.

As in Wales, there is a strong feeling of nationalism in Scotland. A Scottish Parliament with many powers came into being in 1999 and this has been welcomed by most Scots.

Scotland's capital city, Edinburgh, is famed for its ancient castle, perched high on a rock, and the elegant buildings of its Georgian New Town.

Fishing boats leaving from a West Highland fishing port, one of the many harbours around Scotland's coast that take advantage of their proximity to Europe's main fishing grounds.

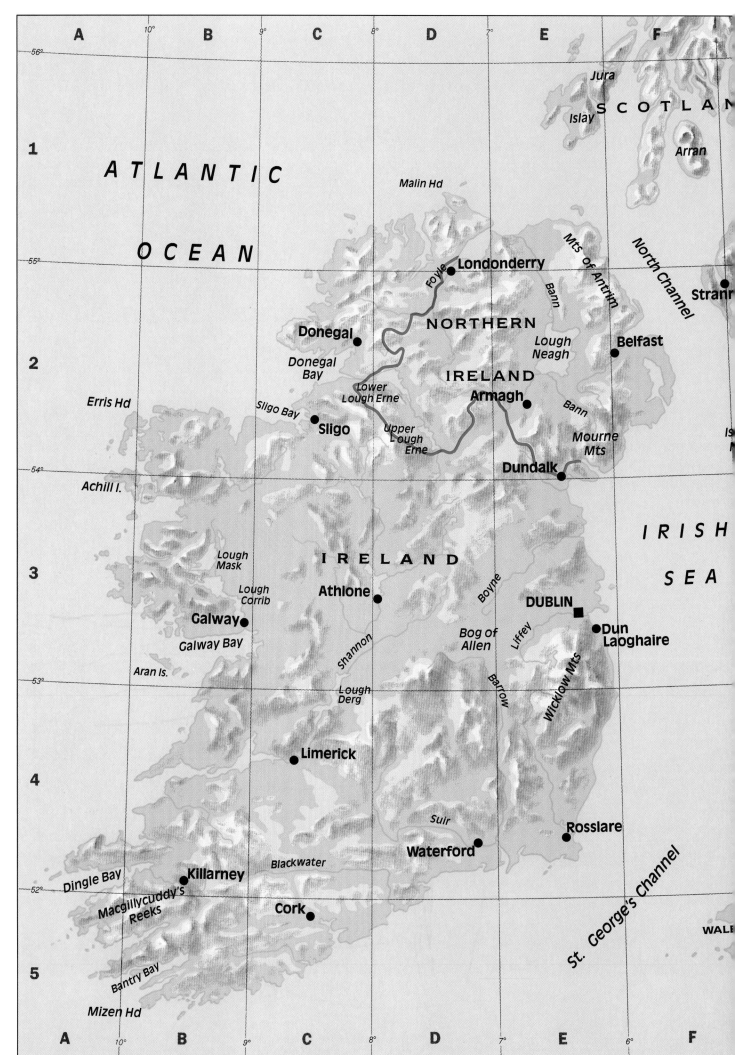

ATLANTIC

OCEAN

Jura

Islay

Arran

SCOTLAN

Malin Hd

Mts of Antrim

North Channel

Foyle

Londonderry

Stranr

NORTHERN

Bann

Donegal

Lough
Neagh

Belfast

Donegal
Bay

Erris Hd

Lower
Lough Erne

IRELAND

Sligo Bay

Sligo

Armagh

Bann

Upper
Lough
Erne

Mourne
Mts

Is
M

Achill I.

Dundalk

IRISH

Lough
Mask

IRELAND

SEA

Lough
Corrib

Athlone

Boyne

DUBLIN

Galway

Bog of
Allen

Liffey

Dun
Laoghaire

Galway Bay

Shannon

Aran Is.

Barrow

Wicklow Mts

Lough
Derg

Limerick

Rosslare

Suir

Dingle Bay

Killarney

Waterford

Blackwater

Macgillycuddy's
Reeks

Cork

St. George's Channel

Bantry Bay

WALE

Mizen Hd

Ireland is the second largest island of the British Isles and is split into two countries, the Republic of Ireland in the south and west, and that part of the United Kingdom known as Northern Ireland, in the northeast.

The island is roughly saucer-shaped, with a central plain surrounded by a rim of mountains, which form high cliffs where the Atlantic Ocean pounds the island in the west. The central plain is low-lying and contains numerous lakes and large areas of bogland. The mountain ranges are rugged, especially in the southwest where the highest peak, Carrauntoohil (1041 metres), is located. The highest peak in Northern Ireland is Slieve Donard (852 metres) in the Mourne Mountains, and the highest in the Republic of Ireland is Carrauntoohil (1041 metres) in the Macgillycuddy's Reeks range in the southwest of the island. The largest lake in Ireland is Lough Neagh (396 square kilometres).

The climate of Ireland is generally mild and moist. It is influenced by the southwesterly winds and the warm waters of the North Atlantic Drift. The climate in the southwest is so mild that many Mediterranean plants can be grown.

The raising of livestock is the most important type of farming in Ireland. There is an extensive area of rich pastureland for the rearing of cattle, sheep and pigs. The Golden Vale of Limerick and Tipperary is one of the finest dairying areas in Western Europe. Production of crops is generally difficult because of the dampness of the climate. Grass and fodder crops are grown in Northern Ireland, and vegetables are grown near the larger towns for the local market.

The main areas of population are found around the two capital cities —Dublin in the south and Belfast in the north. Both cities function as major commercial and industrial centres.

The Killarney Lakes in the mild southwest of Ireland are set in a region famed for its scenic beauty and for the subtropical plants that grow in favoured spots.

In the Republic of Ireland food and drink industries, such as preserving meat, the manufacture of dairy products and brewing, are widespread. Most industry in Northern Ireland is near Belfast, which is well situated at the head of Belfast Lough for the import of raw materials. Northern Ireland now has its own Assembly with many powers in terms of how the country is run and organised.

Tourism is an important industry, especially in Dublin, Killarney and Galway. The beautiful scenery and beaches are the main attractions. Tourism in the north has suffered greatly in recent years due to political unrest.

Trinity College, Dublin, a university founded in 1591, is one of the many fine buildings that grace the elegant streets of Ireland's capital city.

The cliffs of the west coast of Ireland have been formed by the action of the strong breakers of the Atlantic Ocean.

17

FRANCE

France, including the island of Corsica, is the largest country in Western Europe, and although it has a population of over 55 million, it is less densely populated than its neighbours.

It is situated in the northwest of the European mainland and has coastlines on the English Channel, the Atlantic Ocean and the Mediterranean Sea. France has a wide variety of landscapes, ranging from the low-lying areas in the north and southwest to the mountain ranges of the Massif Central and the higher Alps, Jura and Pyrenees. The climate varies from cool and moist in the north to warm Mediterranean in the south.

Vineyards for the production of wine are widespread, and dairy farming produces hundreds of famous French cheeses. France is one of the world's leading manufacturing countries, and most of the industrial towns are located in the northeast near the coal mines.

Along the Mediterranean coast on the Côte d'Azur, tourism is an important industry and, in contrast to the warm beaches, the snow-capped Alps and Pyrenees are popular for winter sports. Mont Blanc on the France-Italy border is the highest point in the Alps.

France is a republic with a president as head of state. The country is divided into 24 regions which are subdivided into 96 departments. The capital city is Paris, and visitors come from all over the world to see its many sights, such as the Eiffel Tower, the Arc de Triomphe, the cathedral of Notre Dame, and many museums and galleries. The city is built on both sides of the river Seine and on two islands in it, the Ile St Louis and the Ile de la Cité. South of Paris is the huge Palace of Versailles, which was built by King Louis XIV in the 17th century.

About 160 kilometres off the southeast coast of France lies Corsica, the country's largest island. The interior of the island is covered in scrub and woodland. The west coast consists of small fishing villages and resorts. The main town, Ajaccio, is the ancient capital and birthplace of Napoleon.

The Arc de Triomphe, built in Paris, the capital of France, in the early 19th century in honour of Napoleon's Imperial Army, is the centrepiece at the junction of 12 of Paris's famous boulevards (avenues), including the Champs-Elysées.

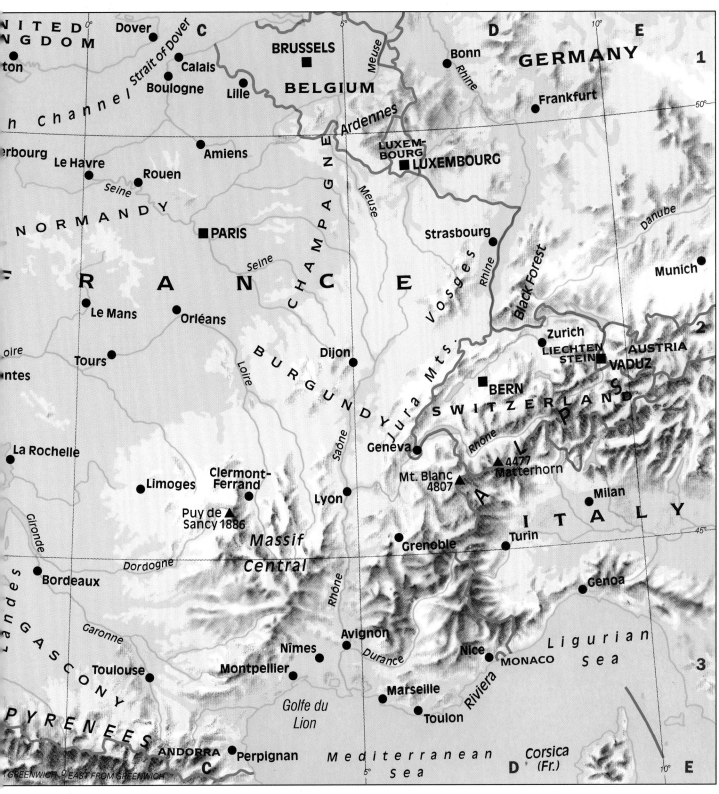

0 100 200 km   0   100 miles

UNITED KINGDOM
Dover
Strait of Dover
C
D
GERMANY
E
1
50°
Calais
BRUSSELS
Bonn
Boulogne
Lille
BELGIUM
Rhine
Frankfurt
Ardennes
Meuse
LUXEM-
BOURG
LUXEMBOURG
erbourg
Le Havre
Amiens
Rouen
Seine
CHAMPAGNE
Meuse
Strasbourg
Munich
Danube
NORMANDY
PARIS
Vosges
Rhine
Black Forest
Seine
Le Mans
Orléans
FRANCE
Zurich
LIECHTEN-
STEIN
AUSTRIA
2
Loire
Tours
Dijon
BURGUNDY
Jura Mts.
BERN
SWITZERLAND
VADUZ
ntes
Loire
Saône
Geneva
Rhône
A   L   P   S
La Rochelle
Clermont-
Ferrand
Limoges
Lyon
Mt. Blanc
4807
4477
Matterhorn
Milan
Gironde
Puy de
Sancy 1886
Massif
Central
Grenoble
Turin
ITALY
45°
Dordogne
Bordeaux
Rhône
Genoa
Garonne
Avignon
Durance
Nice
Ligurian
Sea
GASCONY
Nîmes
Montpellier
MONACO
3
Toulouse
Marseille
Riviera
PYRENEES
Golfe du
Lion
Toulon
ANDORRA
Perpignan
C
Mediterranean
Sea
Corsica
(Fr.)
D
E
GREENWICH 0° EAST FROM GREENWICH
5°
10°

The TGV (Train Grande Vitesse), France's high-speed express train, arriving at Le Mans station, en route to Brest in the far northwest of Brittany.

SPAIN and PORTUGAL

Spain and Portugal are the two largest countries occupying the Iberian Peninsula in the southwestern corner of Europe. The small independent state of Andorra and the British colony of Gibraltar are also part of the peninsula. The Strait of Gibraltar, a strip of water only 15 kilometres wide, separates Spain from the north coast of Africa and links the Mediterranean Sea to the Atlantic Ocean. Spain, the larger of the two countries, includes the Balearic Islands in the Mediterranean Sea, the Canary Islands in the Atlantic Ocean, and the two enclaves of Ceuta and Melilla on the coast of Morocco in North Africa. Mainland Spain is a mountainous country, most of which is made up of a huge plateau known as the meseta. The Pyrenees in the north of Spain form a mountainous boundary with the rest of Europe.

The climate is hot and dry in summer, and mild and moist in winter.

Many people in Spain make their living by agriculture, but in some areas the soils are poor and have insufficient water to produce crops. Cereals are grown on the meseta, and some rice is grown in the valley of the river Ebro, where irrigation is possible. In the lowland areas near the Mediterranean Sea, the growing

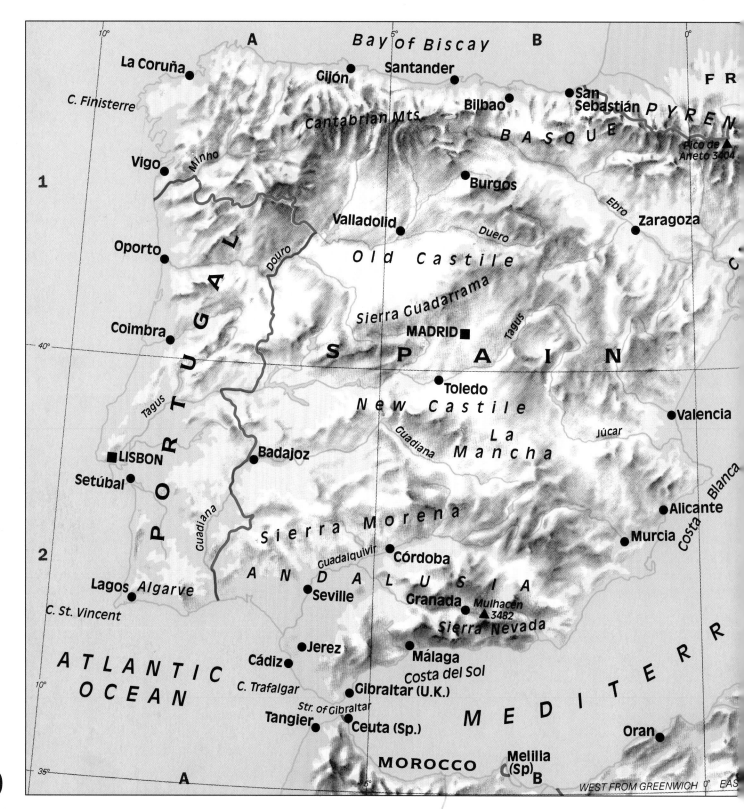

of citrus fruits is important, and grapes for the wine industry are also grown. Spain is the third largest wine producer in Europe.

Spain's Mediterranean coastline has numerous coves and sandy beaches, which attract millions of visitors. It is visited each year by more tourists than any other country in Europe.

Madrid, the capital and largest city in Spain, is located in the centre of the country. Other

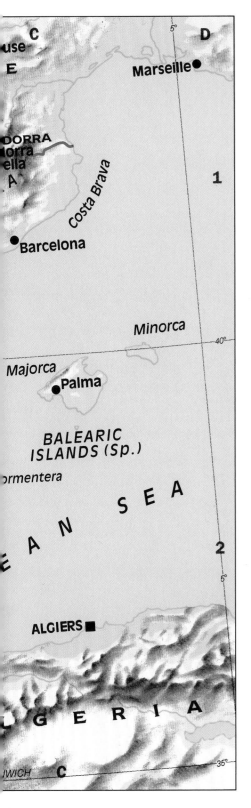

A Spanish coastal resort, one of the many that attract millions of sun-seeking holidaymakers every year to the country's Mediterranean shores.

important cities are Barcelona, Valencia and Seville in the south and east, and Bilbao in the north.

Portugal, to the west of Spain, includes the island groups of Madeira and the Azores in the Atlantic Ocean. Mainland Portugal has a long Atlantic coast. The country is mountainous only in the northeast, where the highlands are divided by deep river valleys. Most of Portugal south of the river

Tagus is low-lying, with flat plains and wide river valleys. In the south, the Algarve has beautiful groves of almond, fig and olive trees fringing the long sandy beaches.

Tourism is a growing industry, and about 13 million visitors travel to Portugal annually.

Portugal's capital, Lisbon, is situated on the northern side of the Tagus estuary, 14 kilometres from the Atlantic Ocean.

The Rossio, the city centre of Lisbon, Portugal, renowned as one of the world's most beautiful capitals, with sun, flowers and palms in abundance.

ITALY and the BALKANS

Italy is a long, boot-shaped peninsula that sticks out into the Mediterranean Sea in southern Europe. The two islands of Sicily and Sardinia are also part of Italy. The Balkan States are the countries of Romania, Bulgaria, Greece, Albania, Slovenia, Croatia, Bosnia and Herzegovina, Macedonia, Montenegro and Serbia, and the European part of Turkey. The oldest country in the region is Greece, with its many islands scattered in the Mediterranean Sea. Greece was the home of one of the world's greatest civilisations, and its main city, Athens, is capital of modern Greece.

The Acropolis, Athens, with its ruined ancient temple of the Parthenon, set high above the modern capital of Greece, is one of the world's most famous sights.

In the north of Italy, the Alps form its border with the rest of Europe. Just south of the Alps is the flat Plain of Lombardy, the most important region for farming and industry. The Apennines are a range of rugged mountains running down the backbone of Italy. Cities such as Rome, the capital, and Naples are located on the narrow coastal strip. The south of Italy is one of the poorest regions in Europe, but recently there has been development in industry and tourism.

Since 1992, Croatia, Slovenia, Bosnia and Herzegovina, Macedonia, Montenegro and Serbia have all broken away from the former Yugoslavia. There has been much political unrest in this region. Albania, a small mountainous country north of Greece, has kept itself isolated for years, but now links are being made with the rest of Europe. Tirana is the capital and main industrial town.

The river Danube is the border between Romania and Bulgaria as it flows east to the Black Sea. Since the end of Communist rule in the area, great changes have taken place. Consumer goods are now being produced, and tourism has been revived at the Black Sea resorts.

0   50   100   150   200 km   0   50   100 miles

D   BUDAPEST ■   Debrecen ●   **E**   **F**   KISHINEV ■   **G**
                                                                                        ● Odessa
                             Oradea ●   MOLDAVIA
H U N G A R Y   Cluj-Napoca ●   **1**
      Balaton   RUSSIAN
                                                                           FED.
   Pécs ●   Mureș   Negoiu   I   A
                                               2548   Brașov
■ ZAGREB   Tisza   Timişoara ●   R   O   Transylvanian Alps
              Danube   45°
C R O A T I A   Sava

              ■ BELGRADE   ■ BUCHAREST   ● Constanța
                      Danube   Craiova ●   Danube
BOSNIA·   Ruse ●
HERZEGOVINA   SERBIA   Morava   BLACK
SARAJEVO   Niš ●   ● Varna   **2**
   Split ●   Durmitor   SEA
              2522   Balkan Mts   30°
         MONTENEGRO   SOFIA ■   Edirne ●
    Dubrovnik ●   Musala   Maritsa Plovdiv ●   Istanbul ●
         L.   2925   B U L G A R I A   Sea of
         Shkodër ●   Skopje ●   Rhodope Mts   Marmara
                           MACEDONIA   Bursa ●   40°
 Foggia ●   TIRANA ■   Néstos
   Bari ●   Thessaloniki ●
     Brindisi ●   Vlorë ●   Límnos
     Taranto ●   Dardanelles   T U R K E Y
              Strait of Otranto   Vólos ●   Lésvos
         Corfu   G R E E C E   İzmir ●
osenza ●   Évvoia   A E G E A N
                                                              S E A   Khíos
                     IONIAN SEA   Pátras ●   ATHENS ■ Sámos
Reggio di   Corinth ● Piraeus
Calabria ●   Peloponnese   CYCLADES   Dodecanese
ania   **3**
                                                                         Rhodes
                                          Sea of Crete   Kárpathos
assero
 S   Crete   Iráklion ●   35°
                                   E   35°   25°   **F**

Venice, the pearl of the Adriatic, is a famous
and historic Italian city built with a network
of canals as its main thoroughfares.

CENTRAL EUROPE

Central Europe extends from the Baltic Sea in the north to the Alps in the south. From the northeastern border of France, it extends through the Low Countries of Belgium, Luxembourg and the Netherlands, Germany, Austria, Hungary, Switzerland, Poland, the Czech Republic and Romania. Its eastern limit is the Carpathian Mountains.

The Alps in the south are the longest and highest range of mountains in Europe and form a natural boundary between Central and Southern Europe. By contrast, the Low Countries are largely flat fertile plains that are densely populated and have many historic centres of industry and Europe's largest port at Rotterdam.

Germany is the largest country in the region. In the north, the landscape consists of flat plains but changes to high mountains in the south. It is crossed by two of Europe's longest rivers: the Rhine (1320 kilometres) and the Danube (2859 kilometres). The Rhine has been an important trade route for centuries. Coal, iron ore and oil are still transported by barge along the Rhine. Germany is one of the world's most successful industrial countries.

The Matterhorn, one of the Alps' most spectacular peaks, rises above the popular winter sports resort of Zermatt in Switzerland.

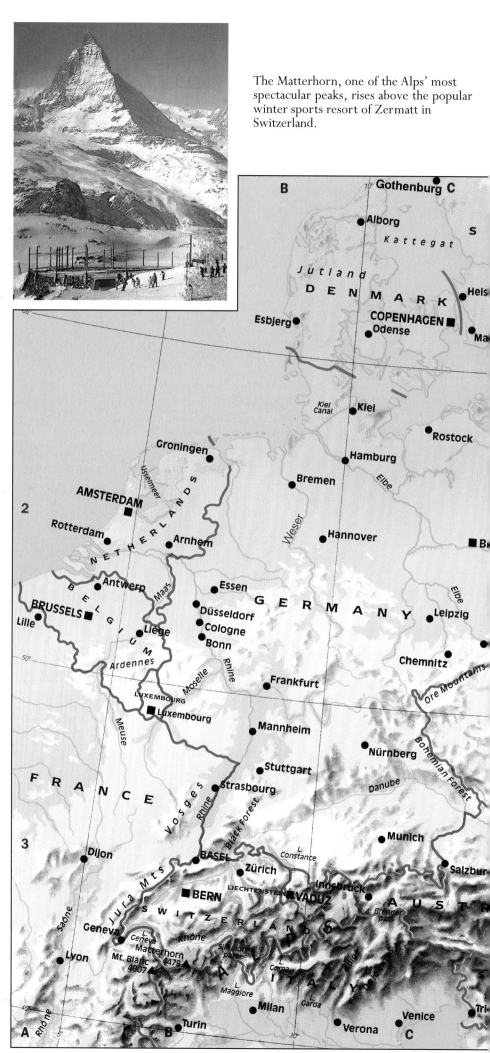

Budapest, like many cities in Central Europe, has an efficient public transport system of modern trams, running throughout Hungary's capital.

0 50 100 150 200km   0 50 100 miles

Austria and Switzerland to the south of Germany are both mountainous. Switzerland is famous for its manufacture of scientific instruments and watches. Tourism is important in both, especially for winter sports.

Poland, the Czech Republic, Slovakia and Hungary have traditionally had close links with the former USSR. Communism is gradually being replaced by more democratic forms of government, and these countries are now

forming closer links with Western Europe. They have always been agricultural, especially along the fertile plain of the river Danube. Poland also has rich coal reserves, as well as large textile, iron and steel and shipbuilding industries.

SCANDINAVIA and the BALTIC

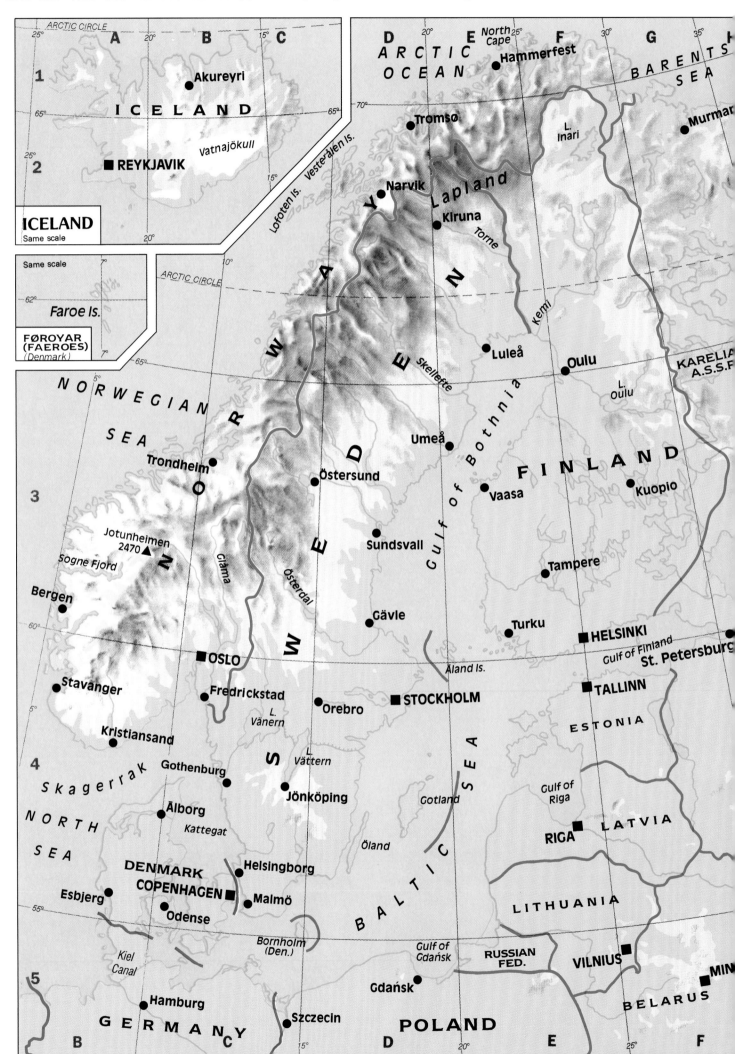

ARCTIC CIRCLE

A **B** **C**

1

Akureyri

I C E L A N D

Vatnajökull

2

■ REYKJAVIK

ICELAND
Same scale

Same scale

Faroe Is.

FØROYAR (FAEROES)
(Denmark)

ARCTIC CIRCLE

D **E** North **F** **G**
Cape

A R C T I C
O C E A N
Hammerfest

B A R E N T S
S E A

Tromsø
L. Inari
Murman

N A R V I K
Lapland
Kiruna
Torne
Karelia
A.S.S.R.

Lofoten Is. Vesterålen Is.

N O R W E G I A N
S E A

Skellefte
Luleå
Oulu
L. Oulu

Trondheim
Östersund
Umeå
F I N L A N D

3

Jotunheimen
2470 ▲
Vaasa
Kuopio

Sogne Fjord
Gläma
Österdal
Sundsvall
Tampere

Bergen
Gävle
Turku
■ HELSINKI
Gulf of Finland
St. Petersburg

OSLO
Åland Is.

Stavanger
Fredrickstad
Orebro
■ STOCKHOLM
■ TALLINN

Kristiansand
L. Vänern
E S T O N I A

S k a g e r r a k

4

Gothenburg
L. Vättern
Gotland
Gulf of Riga

N O R T H
S E A
Ålborg
Jönköping
Öland
RIGA ■ L A T V I A

Kattegat

DENMARK
Helsingborg
B A L T I C
S E A
L I T H U A N I A

COPENHAGEN ■
Malmö

Esbjerg
Odense

Bornholm
(Den.)
Gulf of
Gdańsk
RUSSIAN
FED.
VILNIUS ■
MIN

5

Kiel
Canal
Gdańsk
B E L A R U S

Hamburg
Szczecin
P O L A N D

G E R M A N Y

26

Scandinavia is a region in northern Europe made up of the countries of Norway, Sweden, Denmark, Finland, Iceland, and the Baltic republics of Estonia, Latvia and Lithuania, which are on the eastern coast of the Baltic Sea. Finland, to the east of Sweden, has a frontier with the Russian Federation.

Sweden, with its capital in Stockholm, is the largest country in Scandinavia. The south of the country is mostly low-lying and farms here produce surpluses of dairy products. Crops grown include barley, sugar beet, wheat, oats and potatoes. More than half the country is covered by forest, and Sweden is Europe's largest supplier of wood products and pulp. It is rich, too, in minerals and power sources, and most industry is connected with metals. It is one of the wealthiest countries in Europe.

Norway, with its capital in Oslo, is a sparsely populated and very mountainous country. Its west coast has hundreds of fjords— valleys cut by glaciers and flooded by the sea. The largest is the Sogne Fjord, stretching inland for over 200 kilometres. Very little of the land is suitable for farming but fishing is an important industry. The exploitation of oil from the North Sea has now become a major source of wealth for Norway.

Denmark is a very low-lying country made up of the mainland of Jutland and many islands in the Baltic Sea. Its capital, Copenhagen, is located on the island of Zealand. Agriculture concentrates mainly on dairy farming, and some of the country's main exports are butter, cheese and bacon.

Finland, a mainly low-lying country, has over 60,000 lakes. Three-quarters of the country is covered by forests, and the export of timber is a major source of wealth. The best farmland is in the

The west coast of Norway is indented by numerous fjords, giving the country a total coastline of 21,347 kilometres. Without the fjords, the coastline is a mere 2650 kilometres long.

south. In the far north, reindeer herding is an important activity. Helsinki is the capital and major port, and the home of one-fifth of the total population.

Iceland, an island far out in the Atlantic Ocean, was formed as a result of undersea volcanic eruptions thousands of years ago. Geysers, hot springs and mud volcanoes are continuously active.

The major economic activity in the Baltic republics of Estonia, Latvia and Lithuania is farming, although there is increasing industrial development.

The statue of the Little Mermaid, one of the famous characters created by the Danish author of fairytales, Hans Christian Andersen, sits on a rock in the harbour of the country's capital, Copenhagen.

ASIA: Countries and Capitals

Asia is the largest continent in the world. It extends from the Mediterranean Sea in the west to the Pacific Ocean in the east, and from the Arctic Ocean in the north to the Indian Ocean in the south.

This huge continent is home to more than half the world's population, and it is in Asia that all the world's major religions originated—Buddhism, Christianity, Hinduism, Confucianism, Islam and Judaism.

Asia has a great variety of environments. In the north the frozen wastes of the tundra are found around the shores of the Arctic Ocean. In Southeast Asia near the Equator are the hot wet jungles of the tropical rainforest. Central Asia is mountainous, and it is here in the Himalayan range that the two highest mountains in the world are found. These are Mount Everest (8848 metres) on the China/Nepal border, and K2 (8611 metres) on the China/Jammu and Kashmir border.

The lowest-lying place in the world is also found in Asia, around the shores of the Dead Sea. Asia has some hot, dry desert areas in the southwest and also in the Gobi Desert in Mongolia.

Many of the world's great rivers, including the Yangtze (Chiang Jiang), Ob-Irtysh, Yenesei, Hwang Ho (Huang He), Mekong, Indus, Tigris, Euphrates, Brahmaputra and Ganges flow through Asia.

Not many people live in the regions with extremely cold or hot, dry climates. The main areas of population are found in China and the Indian subcontinent.

In many parts of Asia people live by farming. They may grow just enough food to live on, or they may work on the large plantations that grow tea—as in India and Sri Lanka—or rubber—as in Malaysia —for export. Some Asian countries are highly industrialised. Japan, for example, builds a wide range of products, such as ships, cars and electronic equipment, that are sold throughout the world. Other regions have valuable natural resources, including oil in the Middle East and minerals in India, China and Malaysia.

A Chinese junk sailing in the harbour of Hong Kong, one of the most densely populated cities in the world.

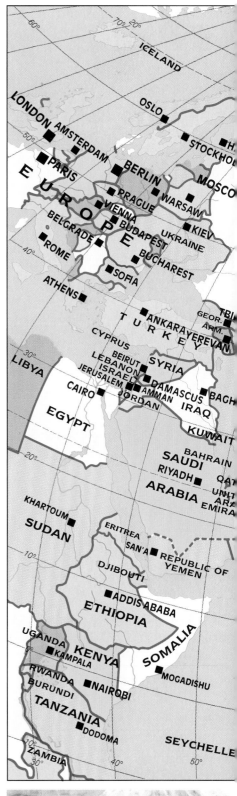

Rice growing, as here in the Philippines, provides the main food crop of South and East Asia.

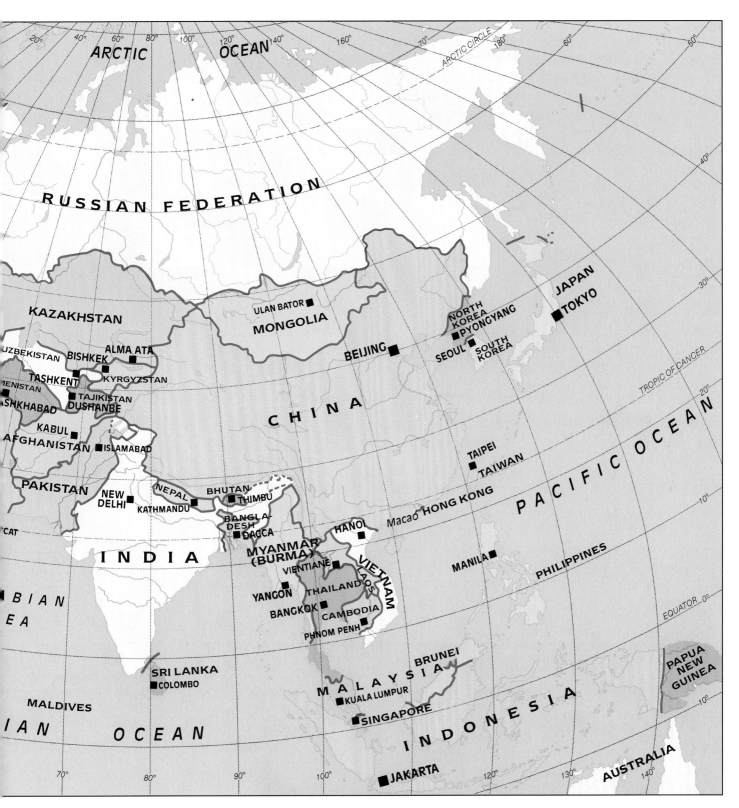

Scale

0 400 800 1200 1600 km   0 200 400 600 800 1000 miles

ARCTIC OCEAN

ARCTIC CIRCLE

RUSSIAN FEDERATION

KAZAKHSTAN

ULAN BATOR ■

MONGOLIA

NORTH KOREA
PYONGYANG

JAPAN
TOKYO ■

UZBEKISTAN
BISHKEK ■
ALMA ATA ■

TASHKENT ■
KYRGYZSTAN

BEIJING ■

SEOUL ■ SOUTH KOREA

MENISTAN
TAJIKISTAN
DUSHANBE ■

SHKHABAD

CHINA

TROPIC OF CANCER

KABUL ■
AFGHANISTAN
ISLAMABAD ■

TAIPEI ■
TAIWAN

PAKISTAN

NEPAL
NEW DELHI ■
KATHMANDU
BHUTAN
THIMBU ■

Macao HONG KONG

PACIFIC OCEAN

BANGLA-DESH
DACCA ■

HANOI ■

'CAT

INDIA

MYANMAR (BURMA)

VIENTIANE ■
VIETNAM
LAOS

MANILA ■

PHILIPPINES

BIAN
EA

YANGON ■
THAILAND

BANGKOK ■
CAMBODIA
PHNOM PENH ■

EQUATOR 0°

SRI LANKA
COLOMBO ■

BRUNEI

PAPUA NEW GUINEA

MALDIVES

IAN OCEAN

MALAYSIA
KUALA LUMPUR ■
SINGAPORE ■

INDONESIA

AUSTRALIA

JAKARTA ■

Mount Everest, the world's highest peak, rises to 8848 metres above
sea level, in the middle of the massive Himalayan Mountains.

RUSSIA and CENTRAL ASIA

Russia, officially known as the Russian Federation, is the world's largest country. It is more than twice the size of Canada and spans two continents. The European part is mainly lowland, and the Ural Mountains form the boundary between Europe and Asia. East of the Urals is Siberia, which stretches to the Pacific Ocean. Much of this region is a huge uninhabited wilderness of pine forests, where the temperatures in winter often drop below -45° Celsius. Siberia is rich in precious stones and oil. The best farmland in Russia is found to the south of the capital, Moscow. During the years of Communist control, farms were either collective or state farms, but private enterprise is now becoming more important. Industry has developed near the

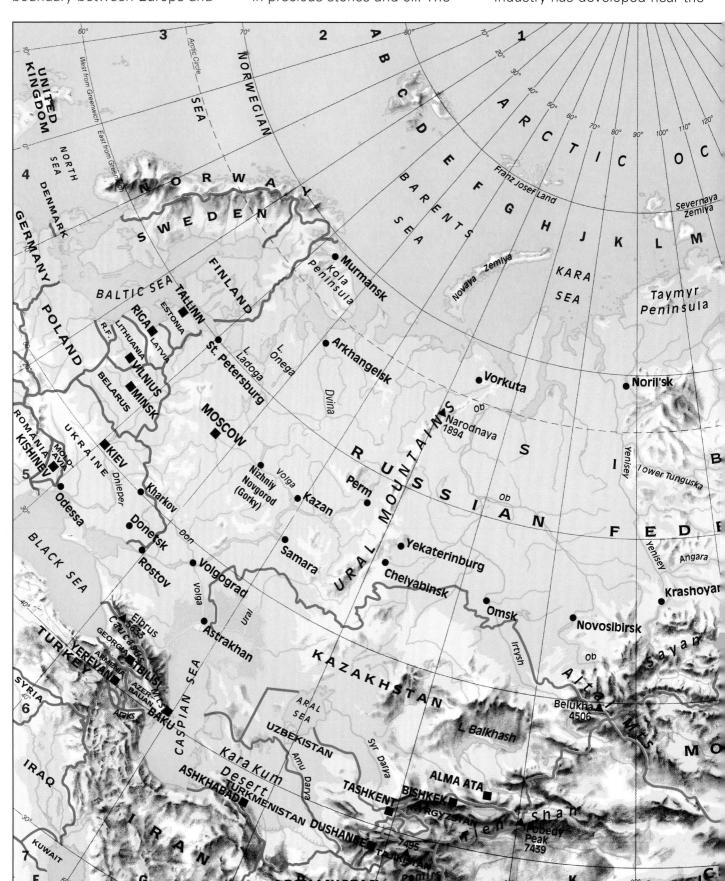

sources of minerals, and in Moscow and cities such as St Petersburg and Nizhniy Tagil.

The large republic of Kazakhstan extends nearly 3000 kilometres from east to west. It is flat in the west and hilly in the east. The climate is very dry, and much of the country is grassland or semi-desert.

In Transcaucasia, three republics—Georgia, Armenia and Azerbaijan—have rich deposits of minerals and oil, especially in the Baku area, from where oil is piped to Batum on the Black Sea.

The four neighbouring Central Asiatic republics south of Kazakhstan—Turkmenistan, Uzbekistan, Tajikistan and Kyrgyzstan—are all semi-desert. Crop growing is only possible where irrigation is available from rivers or lakes.

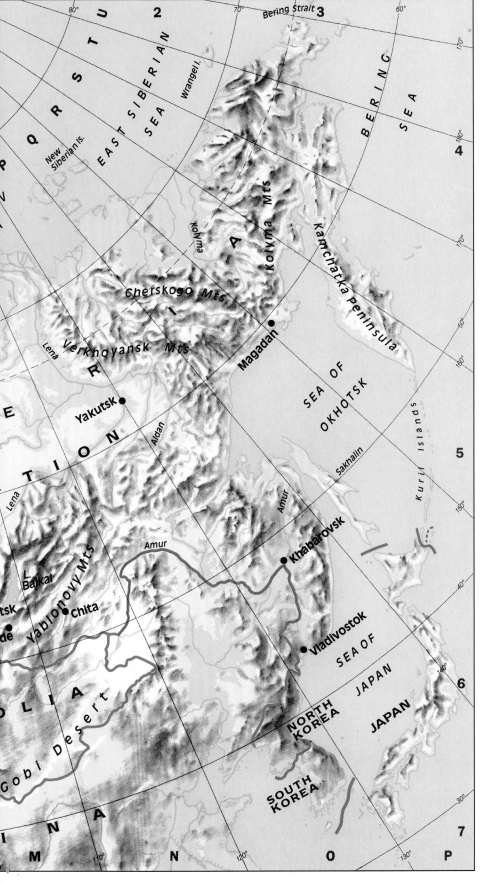

Irkutsk, a Siberian town on the vast grassland plains of Russia, known as the steppes. Although a highly fertile area, the winters here can be very harsh indeed.

St Basil's Cathedral, Red Square, Moscow—the famous domed roofs dominate the capital of the Russian Federation.

31

EAST ASIA

The largest country in East Asia is China, with a population greater than any other country in the world. Over 1000 million people live in China. Most of these people live in the east of the country where the climate is wet and farming land is good. The huge cities of Beijing, Shanghai, Nanjing and Guangzhou are also in the east. In the southwest, the province of Tibet lies in highlands rising to an average height of 4500 metres above sea level. The Himalayas, which contain the world's highest mountain, Mount Everest, stretch along the border with India.

The first Europeans to settle in China were the Portuguese, who established a base at Macao (now Chinese again). Later, the British colony of Hong Kong was established (now also Chinese again). Hong Kong is an important business, banking and trading centre.

To the north of China lies the huge, sparsely populated country of Mongolia. It was formerly inhabited by nomadic herdsmen, but most of the inhabitants have now settled in towns and villages. One-quarter of the population live in the capital city, Ulan Bator.

Japan, situated on the eastern margin of Asia, consists of over 3000 small islands and four main islands—Hokkaido, Honshu,

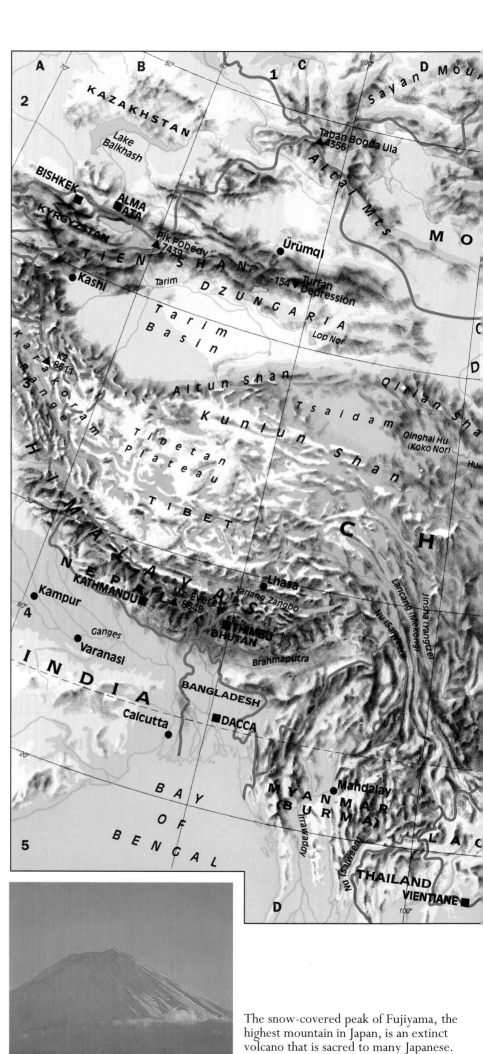

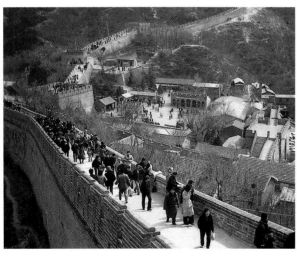

The Great Wall of China is the longest fortification in the world. Built in the 3rd century AD, it extends for over 3400 kilometres and can be clearly seen from spacecraft orbiting Earth.

The snow-covered peak of Fujiyama, the highest mountain in Japan, is an extinct volcano that is sacred to many Japanese.

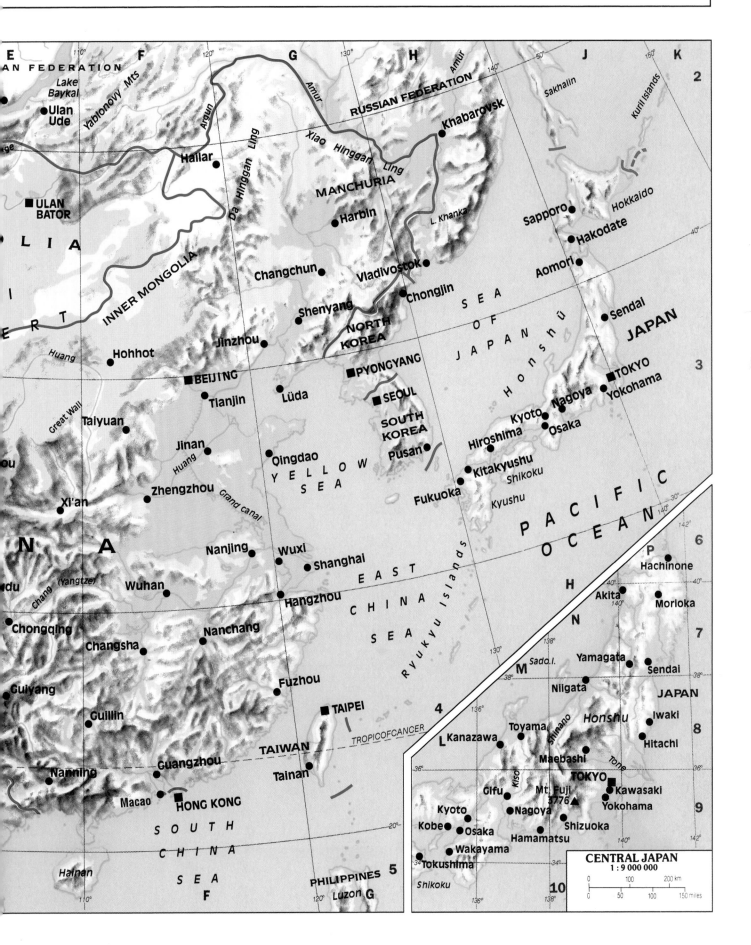

Map labels:

0 200 400 600 800km   0 100 200 300 400 500 miles

AN FEDERATION
Lake Baykal
Ulan Ude
Yablonovy Mts
Argun
Xiao Hinggan Ling
Amur
RUSSIAN FEDERATION
Khabarovsk
Sakhalin
Kuril Islands
Hailar
Da Hinggan Ling
MANCHURIA
ULAN BATOR
L. Khanka
Sapporo
Hokkaido
Hakodate
Harbin
Aomori
Changchun
Vladivostok
SEA
Sendai
INNER MONGOLIA
Shenyang
Chongjin
OF
JAPAN
Huang
Hohhot
Jinzhou
NORTH KOREA
JAPAN
Honshū
BEIJING
Tianjin
Lüda
PYONGYANG
TOKYO
Great Wall
Taiyuan
SEOUL
Kyoto
Nagoya
Yokohama
Jinan
SOUTH KOREA
Hiroshima
Osaka
Huang
Xi'an
Zhengzhou
Grand canal
Qingdao
YELLOW SEA
Pusan
Kitakyushu
Shikoku
PACIFIC
Fukuoka
Kyushu
N A
Nanjing
Wuxi
Shanghai
EAST
du
Chang (Yangtze)
Wuhan
Hangzhou
CHINA
RYUKYU Islands
OCEAN
P
Hachinone
Chongqing
Changsha
Nanchang
SEA
H
Akita
Morioka
Guiyang
Fuzhou
N
Sado I.
Yamagata
Sendai
Guilin
TAIPEI
M
Niigata
JAPAN
TROPIC OF CANCER
Shinano
Honshu
Iwaki
Nanning
Guangzhou
TAIWAN
L Kanazawa
Toyama
Hitachi
Macao
Tainan
Maebashi
Tone
Hainan
HONG KONG
Gifu
Kiso
Mt. Fuji 3776▲
TOKYO
Kawasaki
SOUTH
Kyoto
Nagoya
Yokohama
Kobe
Osaka
Shizuoka
CHINA
Hamamatsu
Wakayama
SEA
Tokushima
PHILIPPINES
Shikoku
Luzon
F
G

CENTRAL JAPAN
1 : 9 000 000
0 100 200 km
0 50 100 150 miles

Kyushu, and Shikoku. The country is mountainous and has many active volcanoes. Japan has an advanced system of agriculture and was once the second largest industrial economy in the world. It depends on the import of raw materials for its highly successful manufacturing industry.

The Korean Peninsula stretches south from the border with China for 1000 kilometres and is separated from Japan by a narrow stretch of water, the Korea-Tsushima Strait. Since 1953, the peninsula has been split into Communist North Korea and non-Communist South Korea.

33

SOUTHEAST ASIA

Southeast Asia comprises an area of mainland Asia and thousands of islands that lie between the Indian and Pacific Oceans.

Countries on the mainland include Burma (Myanmar), Laos, Vietnam, Cambodia, Thailand and Malaysia. These countries all have high mountains, are densely forested and have wide river valleys where rice growing is important. Malaysia is split between the mainland peninsula and the northern part of the island of Borneo, which it shares with Indonesia and Brunei.

Countries made up of islands lie in the South China Sea. The most densely populated country in the region, Indonesia, consists of over 3500 islands, including New Guinea, which it shares with the country of Papua New Guinea. Most Indonesians live on the island of Java, which has rich soils formed from volcanic materials. North of Indonesia, the Philippines are also made up of thousands of islands, the largest of which is Luzon, where the capital, Manila, is located.

In contrast to these scattered island countries are two very small, very wealthy countries. Singapore, at the southern tip of the Malay Peninsula, has always been an important trading centre, and today is a highly efficient industrial country. Brunei, on the northwest coast of Borneo, has become rich because of its deposits of oil.

The climate in Southeast Asia is hot and wet throughout the year, with little seasonal variation. Rain is particularly heavy during the monsoon season. Tropical rainforest is the natural vegetation over most of the region, and in some areas this has been cleared for timber or for growing rice, rubber and tobacco. This forest clearance often leaves hillsides exposed to heavy monsoon rains, which erode the soil, preventing regeneration of both the natural vegetation and crops.

Most of Southeast Asia was once colonised by Europeans, but today all the countries are independent.

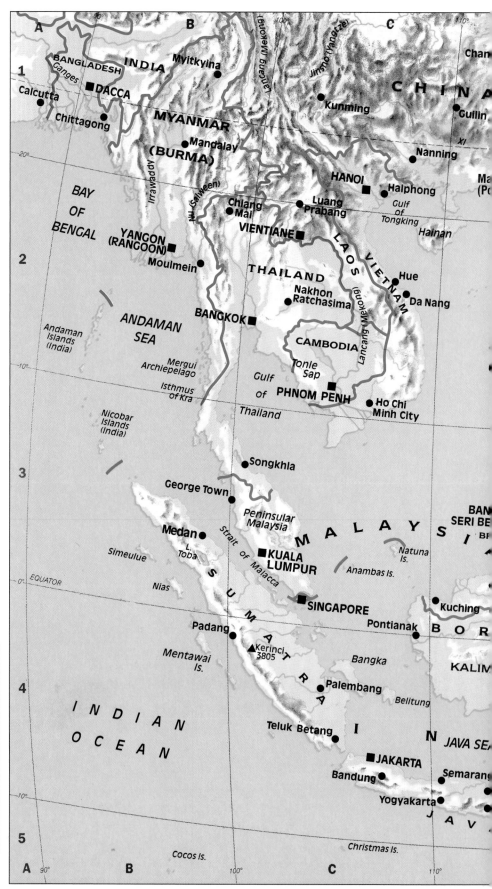

Elephants are used for logging in the teak plantations of northern Thailand.

0   200   400   600   800 km   0   100   200   300   400   500 miles

The Singapore city skyline is dominated by tall skyscraper office blocks, reflecting the wealth of this tiny state's commerce.

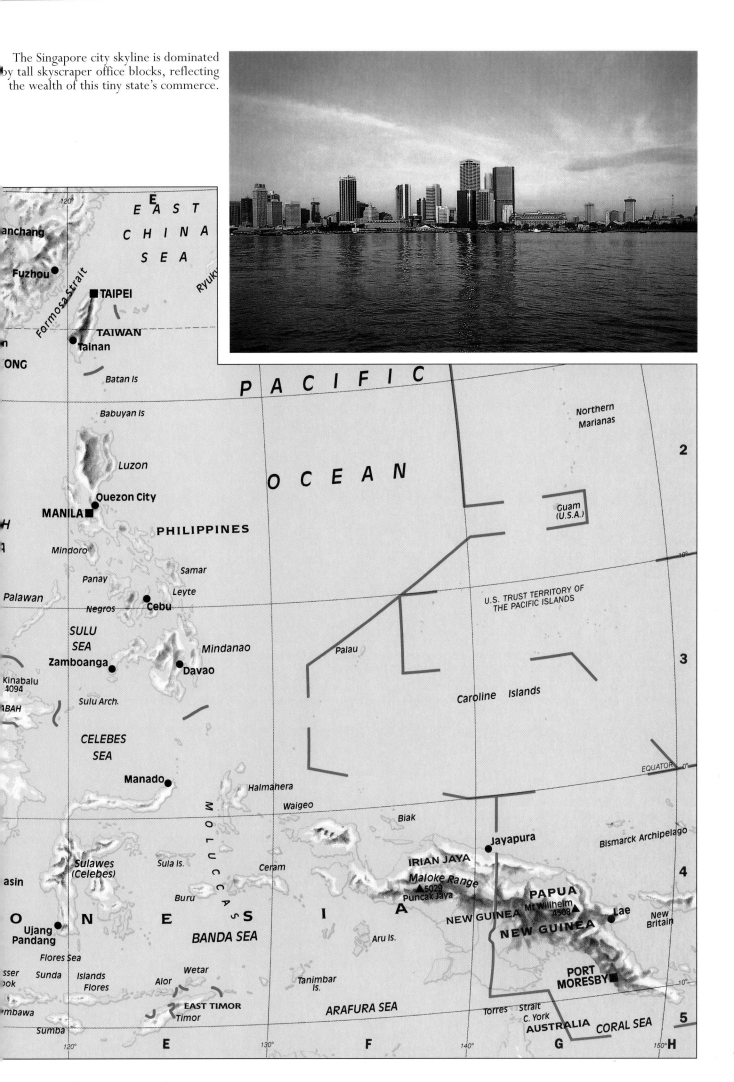

E

E A S T

C H I N A

nanchang

S E A

Fuzhou

■**TAIPEI**

Formosa Strait

Ryuku

TAIWAN

ONG

Tainan

Batan Is

Babuyan Is

P   A   C   I   F   I   C

Northern
Marianas

2

Luzon

O   C   E   A   N

Quezon City

Guam
(U.S.A.)

MANILA■

PHILIPPINES

10°

Mindoro

Samar

Panay

U.S. TRUST TERRITORY OF
THE PACIFIC ISLANDS

Palawan

Leyte

Cebu

Negros

3

*SULU
SEA*

Palau

Zamboanga

Mindanao

*Kinabalu
4094*

Davao

ABAH

Sulu Arch.

Caroline   Islands

*CELEBES
SEA*

EQUATOR   0°

Manado

Halmahera

Waigeo

M O L U C C A S

Biak

*Sulawes
(Celebes)*

Sula Is.

Ceram

Jayapura

Bismarck Archipelago

IRIAN JAYA

asin

Maloke Range

Buru

▲5029
Puncak Jaya

PAPUA

Mt Wilhelm
4508▲

O   **N**   **E**   **S**   **I**   **A**   **NEW GUINEA**   **Lae**   New
Britain

**Ujang
Pandang**

BANDA SEA

Aru Is.

NEW GUINEA

Flores Sea

sser   Sunda   Islands

Wetar

ook

Flores

Alor

*Tanimbar
Is.*

**PORT
MORESBY**■

EAST TIMOR

10°

mbawa

Timor

ARAFURA SEA

Torres   Strait

5

Sumba

C. York

AUSTRALIA   *CORAL SEA*

E   120°   130°   **F**   140°   **G**   150°**H**

35

SOUTH ASIA and the MIDDLE EAST

South Asia is a fan-shaped region separated from the rest of Asia by a huge mountain range, the Himalayas. The largest country is India, and the region is often known as the Indian subcontinent. In fact, seven countries make up South Asia—Afghanistan, Pakistan, Bangladesh, Sri Lanka, Bhutan, Nepal, and India. Over 1000 million people live in South Asia. Although the region has many large cities, such as Calcutta, Bombay and Delhi in India, and Karachi in Pakistan, nearly three-quarters of the people still live by farming the land.

Pakistan was founded in 1947. and Bangladesh in 1972. Afghanistan has long been an area of conflict, and recent war, oppression and drought have left the country impoverished and in ruins.

The Middle East is the area of southwest Asia bordered by the Mediterranean and Red Seas in the west, the Arabian Sea and the Persian Gulf in the east, the Caspian Sea in the north, and by the Indian Ocean in the south.

There is a great variety of landscapes and cultures. The countries bordering the Mediterranean Sea grow citrus fruit, olives and wheat, but farther

Gas flares burning in one of the many oil wells of the Gulf States, which although otherwise mainly desert, are amongst the richest countries in the world.

south, in Saudi Arabia, there are great desert areas. Around the Gulf large deposits of oil were found early in the 20th century, and these now supply the world and have brought wealth to the Gulf States.

Three religions have their roots in the Middle East. Most people are Muslims and the other two religions are Christianity and Judaism. The land of the Bible, ancient Palestine, now lies within modern Israel. There has been much unrest in the Middle East in recent years, with revolution in

Scale bars:
0 200 400 600 800 km
0 100 200 300 400 500 miles

ARAL SEA

E Syr Darya 70° F 80° G 90° H 1

KAZAKHSTAN **ALMA ATA** Tien Shan Turfan Depression 40°

UZBEKISTAN **BISHKEK** Pik Pobedy Tarim Lop Nor Qilian Shan
KYRGYZSTAN 7439 Tarim Basin

TASHKENT Qinghai Hu
(Koko Nor)

ra Kum
esert Samarkand Kashi 2
ENISTAN **DUSHANBE** Cummunism K U N L U N S H A N Jinsho (Yangtze)
Peak 7495 Lancang (Mekong)
ASHKHABAD K2 C H I N A Nu (Salween)
8611 Karakoram Range
Herat Hindu Kush Kashmir Tibet 30°
KABUL Khyber **ISLAMABAD** Lhasa
Pass Peshawar Srinagar
AFGHANISTAN Rawalpindi Yarlung Zangbo **THIMBU**
Kandahar Lahore Amritsar Kanchenjunga **BHUTAN**
Indus Nanda Devi 8585 Brahmaputra Naga Hills
Helmand PAKISTAN 7817 **NEPAL** Mt Everest Imphal
Quetta Multan P u n j a b **KATHMANDU** 8848 3
of Oman Baluchistan Thar Desert Delhi Ganges BANGLADESH TROPIC OF CANCER
NEW DELHI Yamuna Lucknow Ganges **DACCA** **MYANMAR**
Kanpur (BURMA)
Hyderabad Varanasi Calcutta Chittagong
Indus I N D I A 20°
Karachi Rann of Jabalpur
Kutch Ahmadabad Indore Cuttack
Nagpur Mahanadi

A R A B I A N Godavari B A Y
S E A Bombay D e c c a n O F
Pune B E N G A L 4
Krishna Eastern Ghats
Western Madras
Ghats Andaman
Mangalore Islands
Bangalore (India)

Madurai 10°

A N O C E A N Nicobar Islands
C. Comorin (India)
SRI LANKA 5
COLOMBO
MALDIVES 80°

60° E 70° F 80°

Iran, civil war in the Lebanon, wars
between Iran and Iraq, the
invasion of Kuwait by Iraq, and
the Gulf War. There has also been
ongoing conflict between Israel
and its neighbours and in
particular, between Israel and the
Palestinians living in the Palestinian

Administered Territories of the
Gaza Strip and the West Bank
inside Israel.

The Taj Mahal, near Agra in India, is
regarded by many as the world's most
beautiful building.

AFRICA: Countries and Capitals

Africa is a huge continent that stretches about 4000 kilometres north and south of the Equator. It has more countries than any other continent. These countries range from the very small, such as Gambia, to the very large, such as the Sudan. The continent has great variations in climate, landscapes and peoples.

In general, the continent is warm, and only on the highest peaks of Mount Kenya (5200 metres) or Mount Kilimanjaro (5895 metres) is permanent snow found. Around the Equator the dense jungle of the tropical rainforest is typical of the hot wet equatorial climate. Moving north and south from the Equator, the climate becomes drier, and the forest landscape gives way to savanna grasslands. These are home to a wide variety of wild animals, such as giraffes, lions, leopards, elephants, zebras, and gazelles.

As distance from the Equator increases, the climate becomes so dry that very few plants and animals can survive. In northern Africa is the Sahara Desert, the largest area of dry land in the world. It covers about nine million square kilometres and dominates northern Africa. Two smaller deserts, the Kalahari, straddling the Tropic of Capricorn, and the Namib, on the Atlantic coastline of Namibia, are in southern Africa.

The most northern regions in Africa fringe the Mediterranean Sea, into which flows the longest river in the world, the Nile (6685 kilometres). The Nile is fed by streams that flow from the Ethiopian Highlands and the area around Lake Victoria. Each year the Nile floods the farmland along the river valley, and this helps to keep the soils fertile.

Many different groups of people live in Africa, and there are over a thousand different African languages. Arabs and Berbers live in the north. South of the Sahara there are numerous Black African tribes.

During the 19th century, many countries in Africa were colonised by Europeans. Belgium, Britain, France, Germany, Italy, Portugal and Spain all had colonies in Africa. Today all the countries of Africa are once again independent, but many of them have problems, such as widespread poverty, lack of education, drought, disease and famine.

The Sahara is the largest desert in the world, stretching right across northern Africa. Only about one-sixth of the total area is sandy: the rest is mostly rocky or stony.

The savanna (grasslands) of East Africa are the home of the world's largest herds of wild game animals—like these zebras in the Tsavo National Park in Kenya.

The market is a major feature of African life, especially in West Africa, as this one in the Gambia. They are most colourful affairs, with people coming in from the surrounding villages, often from a wide area.

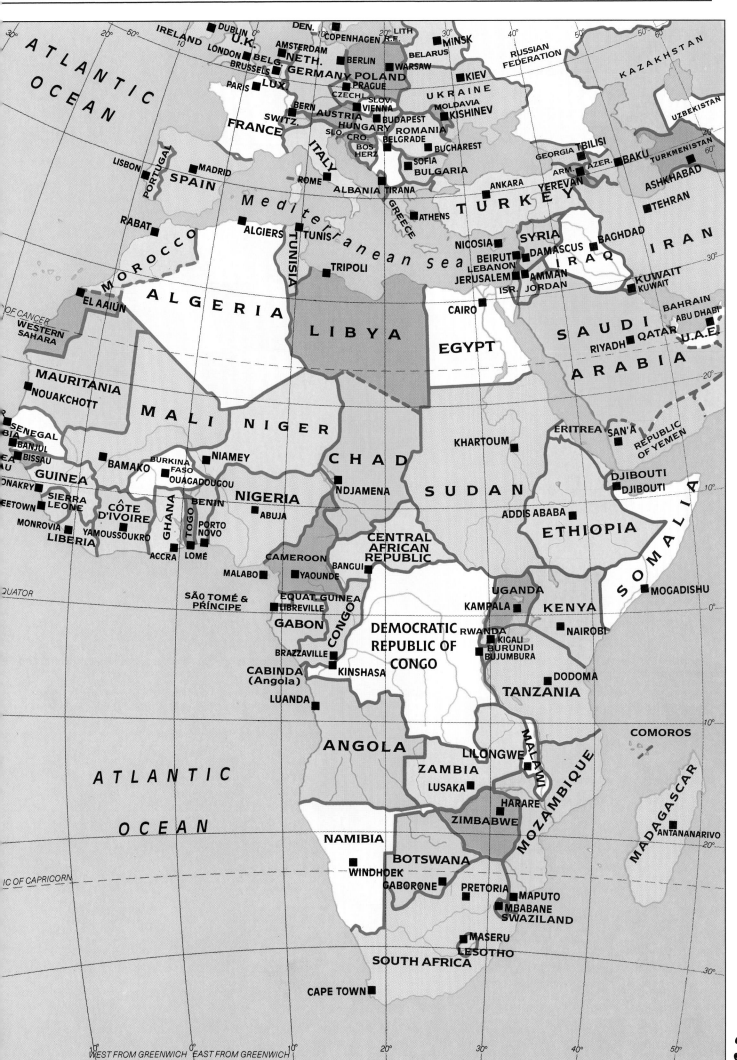

0 400 800 1200 km   0 200 400 600 800 miles

ATLANTIC
OCEAN

IRELAND DUBLIN DEN. COPENHAGEN LITH. MINSK RUSSIAN
U.K. LONDON AMSTERDAM BERLIN WARSAW BELARUS FEDERATION
BELG. NETH. GERMANY POLAND KIEV UKRAINE KAZAKHSTAN
BRUSSELS LUX. PRAGUE CZECH. SLOV. MOLDAVIA KISHINEV UZBEKISTAN
PARIS BERN AUSTRIA VIENNA BUDAPEST ROMANIA GEORGIA TBILISI TURKMENISTAN
SWITZ. HUNGARY BELGRADE BUCHAREST ARM. AZER. BAKU ASHKHABAD
FRANCE ITALY SLO. CRO. BOS. HERZ. SOFIA YEREVAN TEHRAN
PORTUGAL LISBON MADRID SPAIN ROME BULGARIA ANKARA TURKEY IRAN
RABAT ALGIERS TUNIS ALBANIA TIRANA ATHENS NICOSIA SYRIA BAGHDAD
MOROCCO TUNISIA GREECE BEIRUT DAMASCUS IRAQ
EL AAIÚN TRIPOLI JERUSALEM AMMAN KUWAIT KUWAIT BAHRAIN
OF CANCER ALGERIA LIBYA ISR. JORDAN ABU DHABI
WESTERN SAHARA CAIRO SAUDI QATAR U.A.E.
EGYPT RIYADH ARABIA

Mediterranean Sea

MAURITANIA NOUAKCHOTT ERITREA SAN'A REPUBLIC OF YEMEN
MALI NIGER KHARTOUM
SENEGAL BIA BANJUL BAMAKO BURKINA FASO NIAMEY CHAD SUDAN DJIBOUTI DJIBOUTI
BISSAU OUAGADOUGOU NDJAMENA ADDIS ABABA
GUINEA NIGERIA ETHIOPIA
ONAKRY SIERRA LEONE CÔTE D'IVOIRE GHANA BENIN ABUJA
EETOWN YAMOUSSOUKRO TOGO PORTO NOVO CENTRAL AFRICAN REPUBLIC SOMALIA
MONROVIA LIBERIA ACCRA LOMÉ CAMEROON BANGUI
SÃO TOMÉ & PRÍNCIPE MALABO YAOUNDE UGANDA MOGADISHU
QUATOR EQUAT. GUINEA LIBREVILLE KAMPALA KENYA
GABON CONGO DEMOCRATIC REPUBLIC OF CONGO RWANDA NAIROBI
BRAZZAVILLE KIGALI BURUNDI
CABINDA (Angola) KINSHASA BUJUMBURA
LUANDA DODOMA COMOROS
TANZANIA
ANGOLA LILONGWE MALAWI MADAGASCAR
ZAMBIA MOZAMBIQUE ANTANANARIVO
LUSAKA
ATLANTIC
OCEAN HARARE
NAMIBIA ZIMBABWE
BOTSWANA
IC OF CAPRICORN WINDHOEK GABORONE PRETORIA MAPUTO
MBABANE SWAZILAND
MASERU LESOTHO
SOUTH AFRICA
CAPE TOWN

NORTHERN AFRICA

The largest desert in the world, the Sahara, stretches right across northern Africa for almost 5000 kilometres. It covers nine million square kilometres, and daytime temperatures can reach 50° Celsius, while at night they can drop to freezing point. There is very little rainfall, and people can live only around an oasis. The climate is wetter north of the Sahara along the Mediterranean coast, and here citrus fruits, grapes and dates can be grown. Most people live near the Mediterranean or along the banks of the river Nile in Egypt, which also has the 163-kilometre long Suez Canal (completed 1869). Egypt is a farming country, but in Libya and Algeria rich supplies of oil and gas are important sources of wealth.

South of the Sahara, a semi-desert area known as the Sahel stretches across Mauritania, Mali, Niger and Chad. These are among the world's poorest countries. Recently they have suffered terrible droughts, which have resulted in crop failure, famine, disease and death. Most of the countries of

The Pyramids of Giza, just outside Cairo, are amongst the most famous of Ancient Egypt's great treasures. They were built in about 2500BC as tombs for the mummified bodies of pharaohs, or kings.

The palm-lined Atlantic coast of West Africa has few good natural harbours, and many local fishermen ride over the surf and breakers in large canoe-like open boats, as these ones in Ghana.

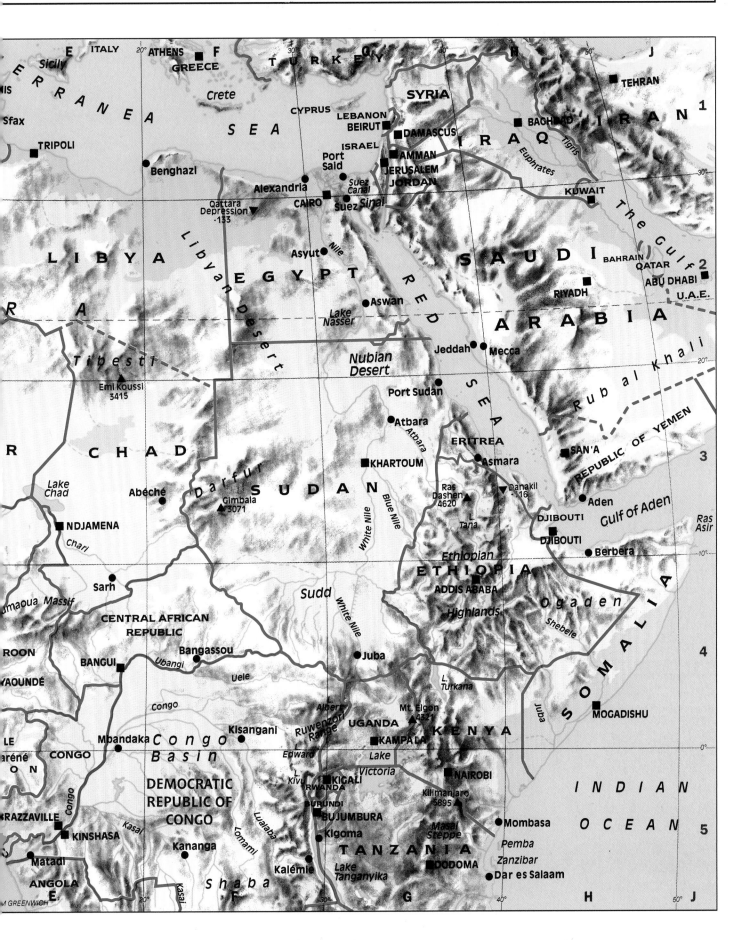

0 200 400 600 800 Km   0 100 200 300 400 500 miles

West Africa were once colonies of European countries such as France and Britain. French and English are still widely spoken. Hot and wet tropical forests are found along the coast of West Africa, and crops such as coffee,

groundnuts and cocoa are grown. Most West African countries depend heavily on the export of raw materials to give them money to import manufactured goods.

The largest country in the region is Nigeria. It was once a

colony of Britain but became an independent country in 1960. It has a very mixed population. Most of the people who live in the north are Muslims, but in the south the people are mainly Christians or follow traditional beliefs.

41

SOUTHERN AFRICA

The southern part of Africa contains a great variety of cultures and landscapes. In the northwest are the great tropical rainforests of the Congo Basin. Small tribes still live in these forests, making clearings to grow crops then moving on when the soil is exhausted. In the northeast are the high plateau lands of Tanzania and the lakes that lie in the southern part of the Great Rift Valley. The tropical grasslands here are called savanna, and crops grown include cotton, coffee, sisal, tea and maize. The savanna supports herds of plant-eating animals such as elephants, gazelles, giraffes and zebras.

South of the Congo Basin cattle are reared on the grasslands. Coffee is grown in Angola, and maize and tobacco in Zambia and Zimbabwe. This region is rich in minerals. Diamonds are found in Angola, huge deposits of copper in Zambia, and coal in Zimbabwe. In the swampy areas of northern Botswana nickel and copper have been found. Farther south lies the Kalahari Desert, which covers part of Botswana and Namibia. South Africa is a wealthy country. Some of the world's richest diamond and gold mines are found here. It is also a major producer of fruit, wheat, cotton and tobacco.

Many years ago, Europeans began to explore and colonise

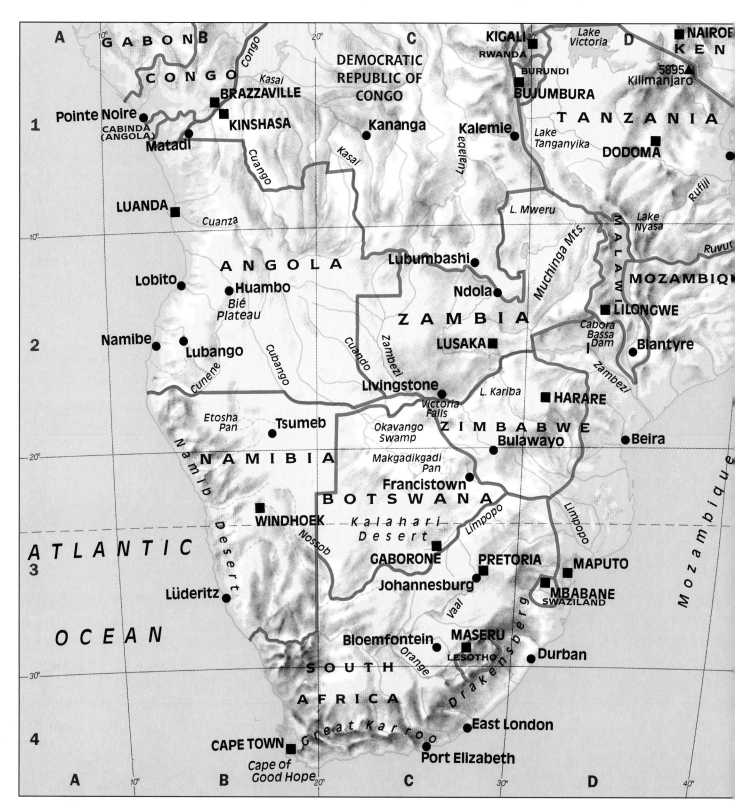

The Victoria Falls, on the Zambesi river where it forms the border between Zambia and Zimbabwe, are known locally as *Mosi-oa-Toenja*, meaning the "smoke that thunders" and referring to the clouds of spray that soar hundreds of metres above the chasm.

E   50°   F

INDIAN   1

SEYCHELLES

OCEAN

—10°

COMOROS

Antsiranana

MADAGASCAR

Toamasina

ANTANANARIVO

—20°

narantsoa

TROPIC OF CAPRICORN

3

50°   F   4

MAURITIUS

—20°   20°

60°

Reunion (France)   MAURITIUS
Same scale

Africa. All the countries they colonised have now been returned to African rule, including South Africa. The Dutch were the first to settle in South Africa. The settlers, later known as Boers, established a base at the Cape of Good Hope in 1652. After the Boer Wars (1899-1902), South Africa came under British rule, but in 1960 it broke its ties with Britain and formalised apartheid—the official government policy of racial segregation. Apartheid ended in the early 1990s and in 1994 South Africa elected its first black president, Nelson Mandela.

Lying off the southeast coast of Africa is the world's fourth largest island, Madagascar. Discovered by Portuguese explorers, it later came under French rule and is now an independent republic. Its main exports are coffee, vanilla, cloves and sugar.

South Africa was once the world's largest producer of gold, much of it being mined in the region around Johannesburg.

The unmistakable flat-topped Table Mountain, which rises above Cape Town, has been a welcome navigational point for sailors over the centuries.

43

NORTH AMERICA: Countries and Capitals

The continent of North America stretches more than 6500 kilometres from the Arctic Ocean to the Gulf of Mexico, and more than 8000 kilometres from the west of Alaska to Newfoundland. Two large countries, Canada and the United States of America, make up most of the land area of North America. Farther south is Mexico and the region known as Central America, which is made up of seven small countries. In the Caribbean Sea, off the southeast coast of the continent, there are many island countries known as the West Indies. Greenland, lying off the northeast coast of Canada, is the world's largest island.

The west of the continent is dominated by the Rocky Mountains, which extend about 4800 kilometres from the Mexican border through the United States and Canada to Alaska. The Rockies are famous for their spectacular scenery. They also have rich natural resources, including forests and minerals such as gold, silver, lead and zinc. The fertile farmlands of the American Great Plains lie to the east of the Rockies. Much of Canada north of the Great Plains is covered by pine forests.

North America's first settlers came from Asia at the time when

Modern Mexico City, the largest city in the world, lies on the site of an ancient city called Tenochtitlán, which was the capital of the Aztec civilisation before the Spanish conquest.

Alaska was still joined to Siberia by a land bridge. The first Europeans began to settle in the 16th century. The next two hundred years saw Britain gaining control of much of northern North America, while the Spanish colonised Central America and the French settled on the east coast of Canada. Following the American War of Independence, 1775–1783, the British lost control, and the country known today as the United States of America was founded. Canada declared independence in 1867.

People continued to emigrate from Europe to North America, and for three hundred years

Europeans shipped black slaves from Africa to work on large farms in the southern states of the United States and in the West Indies. These farms were plantations where cotton, tobacco and sugar were grown.

The people of North America are a mix of many nationalities. In the United States and Canada, the common language is English, although French is also spoken in the province of Quebec. In Mexico and most of Central America, Spanish is the main language spoken.

Monument Valley lies in the arid semi-desert southwest of the USA, and is characterised by rock formations like these buttes and mesas.

The busy Interstate highways cross America from coast to coast and up and down this vast continent.

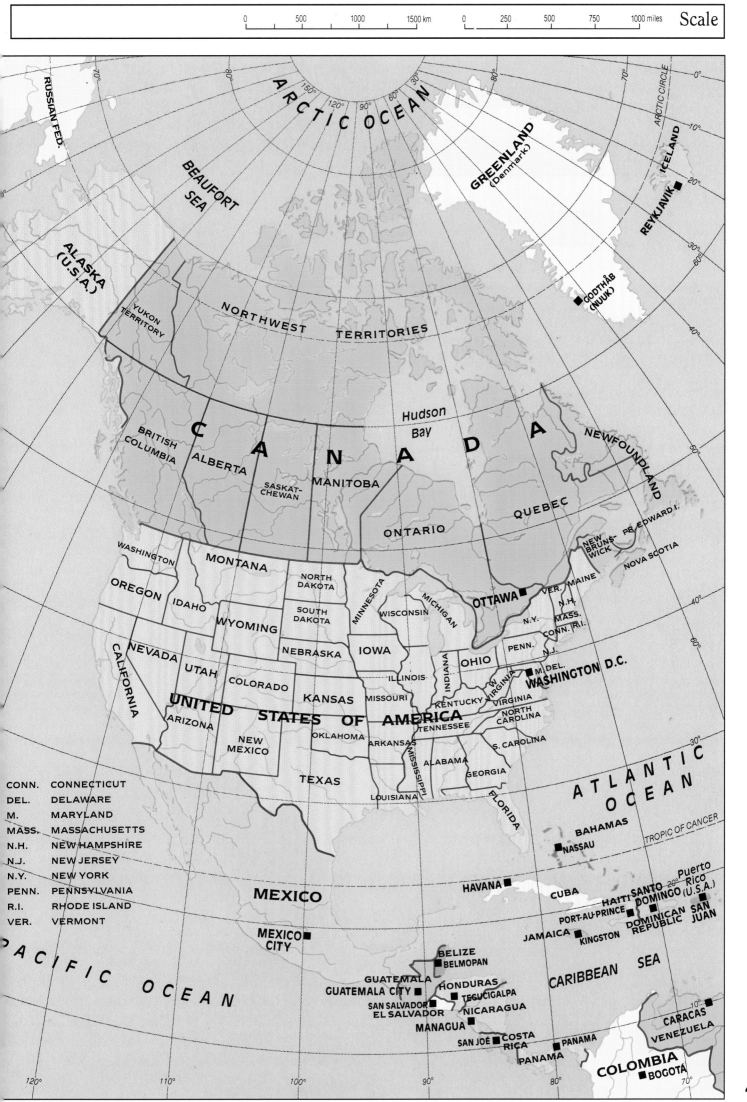

Scale

| 0 | 500 | 1000 | 1500 km |
| 0 | 250 | 500 | 750 | 1000 miles |

ARCTIC OCEAN

RUSSIAN FED.

GREENLAND
(Denmark)

BEAUFORT
SEA

ICELAND

REYKJAVIK

ALASKA
(U.S.A.)

GODTHÅB
(NUUK)

YUKON
TERRITORY

NORTHWEST   TERRITORIES

C A N A D A

Hudson
Bay

NEWFOUNDLAND

BRITISH
COLUMBIA

ALBERTA

SASKAT-
CHEWAN

MANITOBA

QUEBEC

NEW
BRUNS-
WICK

PR. EDWARD I.

NOVA SCOTIA

ONTARIO

WASHINGTON

MONTANA

NORTH
DAKOTA

MINNESOTA

MICHIGAN

OTTAWA

VER.

MAINE

N.H.

OREGON

IDAHO

SOUTH
DAKOTA

WISCONSIN

N.Y.

MASS.

CONN. R.I.

WYOMING

NEBRASKA

IOWA

OHIO

PENN.

N.J.

NEVADA

UTAH

COLORADO

ILLINOIS

INDIANA

W.
VIRGINIA

M. DEL.

WASHINGTON D.C.

CALIFORNIA

KANSAS

MISSOURI

KENTUCKY

VIRGINIA

UNITED   STATES   OF   AMERICA

ARIZONA

NEW
MEXICO

OKLAHOMA

ARKANSAS

TENNESSEE

NORTH
CAROLINA

S. CAROLINA

MISSISSIPPI

ALABAMA

GEORGIA

TEXAS

LOUISIANA

FLORIDA

ATLANTIC
OCEAN

CONN.   CONNECTICUT
DEL.   DELAWARE
M.   MARYLAND
MASS.   MASSACHUSETTS
N.H.   NEW HAMPSHIRE
N.J.   NEW JERSEY
N.Y.   NEW YORK
PENN.   PENNSYLVANIA
R.I.   RHODE ISLAND
VER.   VERMONT

BAHAMAS

NASSAU

TROPIC OF CANCER

MEXICO

HAVANA

CUBA

HAITI

SANTO
DOMINGO

Puerto
Rico
(U.S.A.)

PORT-AU-PRINCE

DOMINICAN
REPUBLIC

SAN
JUAN

MEXICO
CITY

JAMAICA

KINGSTON

BELIZE

BELMOPAN

CARIBBEAN   SEA

GUATEMALA

GUATEMALA CITY

HONDURAS

TEGUCIGALPA

SAN SALVADOR
EL SALVADOR

NICARAGUA

CARACAS

VENEZUELA

PACIFIC   OCEAN

MANAGUA

SAN JOÉ
COSTA
RICA

PANAMA

PANAMA

COLOMBIA

BOGOTÁ

45

CANADA

Canada is a huge country, more than forty times bigger than the United Kingdom. It covers most of the northern part of the North American continent. It does not, however, have a large population compared with its neighbour, the United States of America. The north of the country is almost empty. The far north is in the Arctic, where the climate is so cold that only plants such as mosses and lichens can survive the long winters. Farther south are huge areas of coniferous forests. Most of the population live in the southeast, in towns and cities around the Great Lakes and the St Lawrence river. Ottawa is the capital of Canada, but Toronto and Montreal are much larger cities.

In the centre of Canada, between the Great Lakes and the Rocky Mountains, lie the prairies—flat plains extending for thousands of kilometres, from the province of Alberta to the province of Manitoba. Wheat is grown in the fertile soils of the prairies, and cattle are reared on the grasslands.

West of the prairies are the high Rocky Mountains, visited by tourists for skiing in winter and for their spectacular scenery in summer.

The Pacific coast is the warmest part of Canada in winter. Salmon are caught in the rivers here and tinned for export.

The first inhabitants of Canada were the Indian and Eskimo (Inuit) peoples. The French were the first European settlers. They founded a community on the coast of Nova Scotia and later sailed up the St Lawrence river to the site that is now the city of Quebec. The influence of the French has always been strong, and many people in the province of Quebec still speak French. The British followed the French and settled in Newfoundland. Canada is now an independent country and a member of the Commonwealth.

Toronto, on Lake Ontario, is Canada's largest city, and is dominated by the CN Tower, one of the world's tallest buildings.

Canada is rich in minerals, which range from asbestos to zinc. The most valuable products are oil, natural gas, coal and iron ore. Industry is highly mechanised and includes car manufacture, petroleum products, food and metal processing. Ontario has most of the car factories, is the main steel producer and has important aircraft and machinery industries. Quebec has textile, paper, clothing and chemical industries.

Tourism has become important to the economy. The Niagara Falls and the Rocky Mountains are world famous, and many visitors come to the historic cities of Quebec and Montreal and to the modern Toronto.

The prairies of mid-west Canada are fertile grasslands that today are turned over to large-scale grain cultivation.

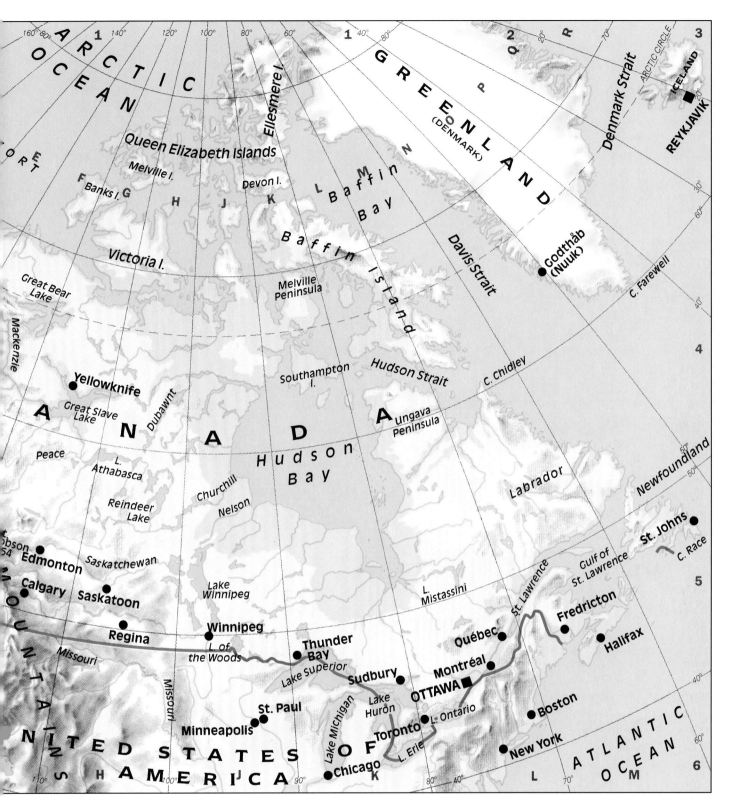

0   200   400   600   800km   0   200   400   600 miles

ARCTIC OCEAN

Queen Elizabeth Islands

Ellesmere I.

GREENLAND
(DENMARK)

Melville I.

Banks I.

Devon I.

Baffin Bay

Denmark Strait

Arctic Circle

ICELAND

REYKJAVIK

Victoria I.

Baffin Island

Great Bear Lake

Melville Peninsula

Davis Strait

Godthåb (Nuuk)

C. Farewell

Mackenzie

Yellowknife

Southampton I.

Hudson Strait

C. Chidley

Great Slave Lake

Dubawnt

Ungava Peninsula

C A N A D A

Peace

L. Athabasca

Churchill

Hudson Bay

Labrador

Newfoundland

Reindeer Lake

Nelson

Edmonton

Saskatchewan

L. Mistassini

St. Johns

C. Race

Calgary

Saskatoon

Lake Winnipeg

St. Lawrence

Gulf of St. Lawrence

Fredricton

Regina

Winnipeg

Thunder Bay

Québec

Halifax

Missouri

L. of the Woods

Lake Superior

Sudbury

Montréal

OTTAWA

Missouri

St. Paul

Lake Michigan

Lake Huron

Toronto

L. Ontario

Boston

Minneapolis

U N I T E D   S T A T E S   O F

L. Erie

New York

ATLANTIC OCEAN

A M E R I C A

Chicago

An Eskimo husky-led sleigh team on a seal hunt in Canada's frozen far north.

THE UNITED STATES OF AMERICA and MEXIC

The United States, the second largest country in North America, is one of the world's richest nations and has a population of almost 270 million. It is made up of 50 states, 48 of which are linked together in the area lying between Canada and Mexico. The other states are Alaska, situated northwest of Canada, and Hawaii in the Pacific Ocean. The national capital is Washington DC (DC stands for District of Columbia).

Two great mountain ranges dominate the country, the Rocky Mountains, or Rockies, in the west, and the Appalachians in the east. Between the two lie the fertile, flat lands of the Great Plains, which are crossed by many rivers. The largest of these rivers is the Mississippi, which with its main tributary, the Missouri, is the fourth longest river in the world.

The four stone carvings of the heads of American presidents George Washington, Thomas Jefferson, Abraham Lincoln and Theodore Roosevelt on Mount Rushmore, South Dakota.

The Golden Gate Bridge, which spans the opening where the Pacific Ocean enters San Francisco Bay, is often covered in mist as cold air from the ocean meets the warm land of California.

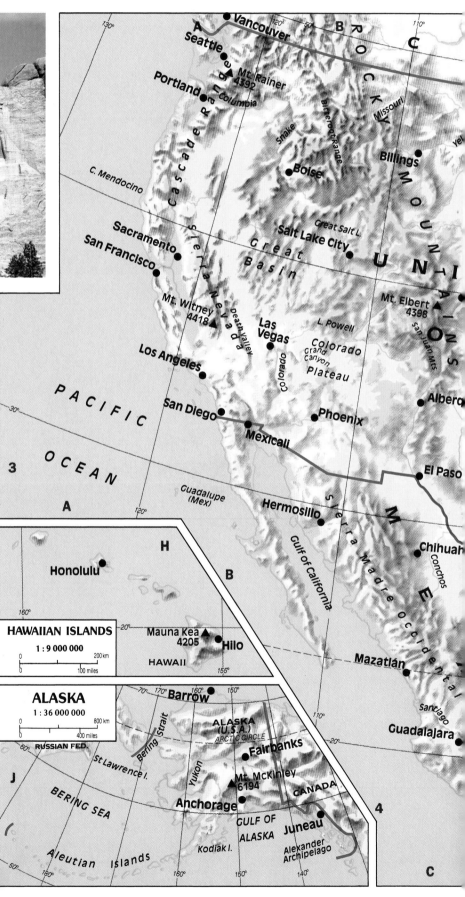

The Great Lakes, Superior, Michigan, Huron, Erie and Ontario, in the northeast form part of the border with Canada. They are often frozen for several months each winter. In contrast, the state of Florida in the southeast has a subtropical climate. Large cities are found throughout the United States. The largest, New York, with its famous skyscraper skyline, is the financial and trade centre of the country, its leading port, and an important manufacturing centre.

Mexico, lying south of USA, is a land of volcanic mountains and high plateaux. It has a fast-growing population, and its capital, Mexico City, is the largest city in the world. Many of Mexico's 85 million people are subsistence farmers, while much wealth comes from oil, gas and silver extraction.

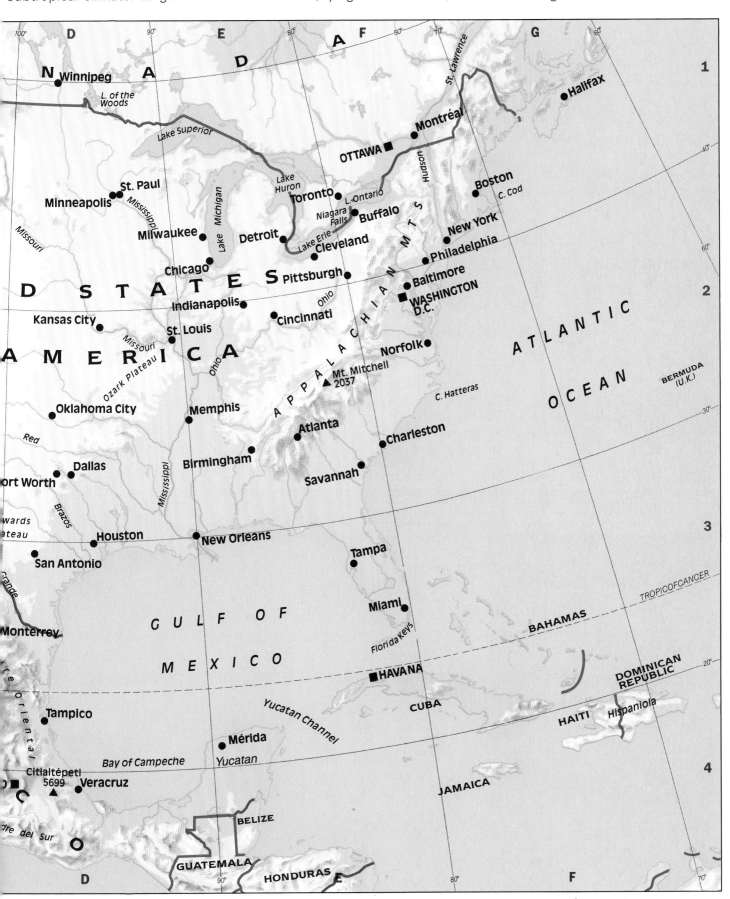

CENTRAL AMERICA and the CARIBBEAN

Central America is a narrow strip of mountainous land joining the continents of North and South America. It is bordered to the west by the Pacific Ocean, and to the east by the Gulf of Mexico and the Caribbean Sea. Between the Mexican border and South America, there are seven small countries—Guatemala, Belize, Honduras, El Salvador, Nicaragua, Costa Rica, and Panama. At the narrowest point in Central America the Panama Canal, 64 kilometres long, forms the main routeway from the Atlantic Ocean to the Pacific Ocean.

In the Caribbean Sea there are hundreds of islands, which are sometimes called the West Indies. These stretch in a chain from the Bahamas, just off the coast of Florida, to Trinidad, just off the coast of South America.

In the lowland areas around the coasts of Central America the climate is hot and humid, and very unhealthy. As a result, many of the main towns are located in the cooler mountainous regions. In much of Central America forests have been cleared so that crops such as coffee and bananas can be grown. In Belize, however, most of the country is still tropical rainforest. Belize, a British colony until 1981, is very different from its neighbours. It has a population of only 235,000 people and the spoken language is English, not Spanish as in the other countries of mainland Central America.

The Caribbean islands are hot, sunny and surrounded by clear blue waters. Most of the island people have European or African ancestors. They are generally poor and earn their living from farming, although tourism is increasingly becoming an important money-earner. Most tourists are Americans or Europeans.

The climate in the Caribbean is ideal for the growing of fruit, sugar cane and coffee, although sometimes hurricanes rage through the region, causing great damage to crops and people's homes. Cuba is the largest island and one of the world's biggest sugar producers. It also grows

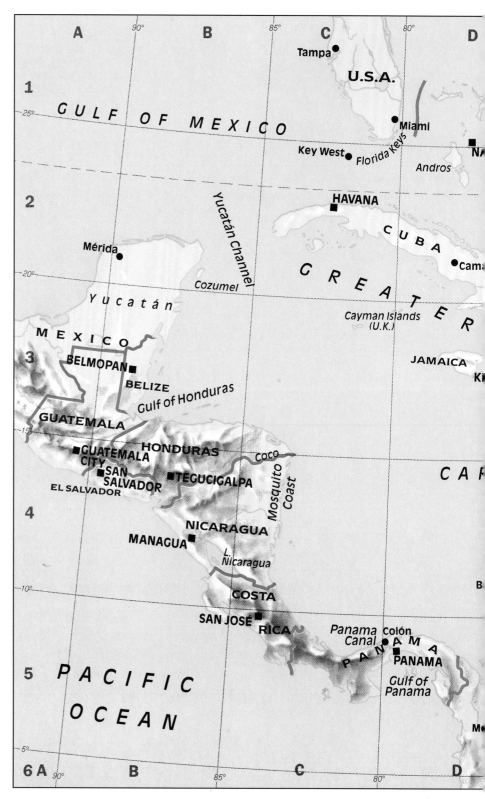

The tropical palm-lined beaches of the Caribbean Islands have become popular holiday destinations for increasing numbers of tourists from North America and Europe.

The Panama Canal was built early in the 20th century to allow ships to pass between the Atlantic and Pacific Oceans, without the long and rough voyage by way of Cape Horn. It is 64 kilometres long.

tobacco, although its traditional markets in the former USSR and Eastern Europe have been eroded. It also has valuable deposits of nickel and iron ore.

Jamaica grows sugar cane and bananas on the farmland around the edges of the island. It has a large population, and as a result many Jamaicans have to emigrate to find work.

Farther south, the islands of Barbados and Trinidad both produce sugar and sugar products, but the main export of Trinidad is oil.

Many of the Caribbean islands are popular stop-off points for cruise liners, and islands such as St Lucia, Barbados, Trinidad and Tobago have become important tourist destinations.

Sugar cane-growing is a major industry of the Caribbean, especially on the island of Cuba, even though many of its former markets in Eastern Europe have disappeared.

SOUTH AMERICA: Countries and Capitals

South America is divided into twelve independent countries and one overseas department of France. The continent was colonised by the Spanish and Portuguese between the 15th and 19th centuries. The people of South America are descended from American Indians, Europeans and Africans. Spanish is the language of all the countries except Brazil, where Portuguese is spoken.

Brazil covers nearly half of the whole continent, and over half of all South Americans live in Brazil. Most of the population live on or near the coast. The capital city is Brasilia, and the commercial centre is Rio de Janeiro. Brazil is rich in minerals, especially high-grade quartz crystal and iron ore.

The three small countries of Guyana, Surinam and French Guiana lie to the north of Brazil and are covered by dense forest. Timber is a major export.

Argentina is the second largest country in South America. It has huge areas of grasslands, called the pampas, where sheep and cattle are grazed. Argentina was once a wealthy country but its economy has seen a dramatic downturn in recent years. The capital, Buenos Aires, has a population of nearly 3 million.

Uruguay and Paraguay are also agricultural nations. Most of Uruguay is used for grazing sheep and cattle, and Paraguay's most important export crop is cotton. Paraguay is a landlocked country, which makes trading difficult.

The Andean countries of South America include Venezuela, Colombia, Ecuador, Peru and Bolivia. Venezuela is one of the richer countries in South America because of its deposits of oil found under the waters of Lake Maracaibo.

In Colombia, coffee-growing is extremely important, and coffee is a major export. Colombia also has rich mineral deposits and produces much of the world's diamond output.

In Ecuador, Bolivia and Peru, most of the population live on high plateaux between the mountains. Bolivia has deposits of tin and oil but lacks funds for their extraction.

Chile stretches like a backbone down the Pacific coast of South America, with the bulk of its population living in the centre of the country. It is rich in natural resources such as coal and copper.

The Amazon rainforest covers an area larger than Western Europe and is home to more than one-fifth of the world's animal and plant species. It is under threat of deforestation.

The ruins of the spectacular Machu Picchu settlement in the Andes of Peru remind us of the wealth of the former Inca civilisation that flourished in South America until it was destroyed by the 16th-century Spanish conquistadors.

Llamas are the South American "pack horse", used by nomadic Indians on the rough and steep routes through the high Andes Mountains.

Scale

0 200 400 600 800 1000 1200 km

0 200 400 600 800 1000 miles

80°   70°   60°   50°   40°

Martinique (Fr.)
Neth.   ST. LUCIA
Antilles   ST. VINCENT   BARBADOS
            GRENADA
CARACAS   TRINIDAD
PORT OF SPAIN   AND TOBAGO

PANAMA
PANAMA

VENEZUELA   GEORGETOWN
                PARAMARIBO
BOGOTÁ   GUYANA   SURINAM   CAYENNE
                        FRENCH
COLUMBIA   GUIANA

EQUATOR
QUITO   0°
ECUADOR

PERU

                                            10°

LIMA

BOLIVIA
LA PAZ   BRASÍLIA

SUCRE

                                            20°
            PARAGUAY

OF CAPRICORN   30°
PACIFIC   ASUNCION

OCEAN   ARGENTINA

                        URUGUAY   30°
SANTIAGO   MONTEVIDEO
        BUENOS AIRES   ATLANTIC

                                OCEAN

                                            40°

                Falkland Is.
                (U.K.)
Tierra
del Fuego   South Georgia   50°
                            (U.K.)

90°   80°   70°   60°   50°   40°   30°   20°

53

SOUTH AMERICA

Great mountain ranges, thick forests, wide plains and desert are all features of the South American continent. Its most striking feature is the great mountain chain of the Andes, which runs from north to south through the whole continent, a distance of more than 8000 kilometres. In many regions the Andes are still rising, and it is one of the most active places on the earth's crust. Hundreds of the mountains in the range are volcanoes. Most notable examples are Huascaran in Peru and Cotopaxi in Ecuador, at 5896 metres the highest active volcano in the world.

The highest navigable lake in the world, Lake Titicaca, is located in the Andes on the border of Peru and Bolivia. Travelling is not easy in these mountains as roads and railways are expensive and difficult to build.

Many streams and rivers that rise in the Andes join to form the great Amazon and Orinoco rivers. The largest tropical rainforest in the world is found in the Amazon Basin. Few people live in this area as the hot wet climate and the difficulties of travelling through the forest discouraged settlement. Trees are now being cut down to build roads and to clear land for

Rio de Janeiro, dominated by its famous Sugar Loaf Mountain, is one of Brazil's largest cities, renowned for its slums, its beaches, and its annual carnival.

farming. Unfortunately, the soils quickly lose their fertility after the trees are cleared, and the land is left abandoned.

In the southeast of the continent, lying just east of the mountains, are the flat grassland plains called the pampas. The soils here are deep and very fertile, ideal for growing wheat. The grasslands are used to graze millions of cattle and sheep. In some places, the cattle are herded by the *gauchos*, South American cowboys.

In the north of Chile is the Atacama Desert. The area

contains some of the driest places on earth. Parts of the desert have been without rain for 400 years. It is, however, rich in nitrates, which are exported for use in making fertilisers or medical drugs.

Conditions in the south of Chile and Argentina could not be more different. The almost uninhabited region of Patagonia in southern Argentina is a vast cold desert which is mostly barren except in the river valleys.

Right at the tip of the continent is Cape Horn, where fierce storms rage for much of the year. The first captain to sail round Cape Horn was the Portuguese explorer Ferdinand Magellan in 1520.

Lying off the coast of Argentina are the Falkland Islands, known as the Islas Malvinas to the Argentinians. They comprise two large and about 200 small islands and are a British crown colony. The islands were invaded by Argentina in April 1982 but recaptured by a British expeditionary force in June 1982.

The Pampas of Argentina are vast fertile grassland plains where large numbers of cattle are reared by the *gauchos* (South American cowboys).

Scale

| 0 | 200 | 400 | 600 | 800km | 0 | 200 | 400 | 600 | 800miles |

Barranquilla · Maracaibo · CARACAS
PANAMA
PANAMA
L. Maracaibo
Manizales
Medellín
BOGOTA
COLOMBIA
QUITO
ECUADOR Cotopaxi
Chimborazo
Guayaquil
Iquitos
Marañón
Chimbote
P E R U
Callao LIMA
Cuzco
Arequipa
Arica
Antofagasta
Ojos del Salado 6863
Valparaíso SANTIAGO
Valdivia
Puerto Montt
Chiloé I.

VENEZUELA
Orinoco
Angel Falls
GUYANA
Roraima 2810
SURINAM
Ciudad Bolívar
GEORGETOWN
PARAMARIBO
CAYENNE
FRENCH GUIANA

A T L A N T I C

O C E A N

2

EQUATOR

Negro
Amazon
Belém
Manaus
Madeira
Purus
Tapajos
V A S T
E L
S E L
B R A Z I L

Fortaleza

3

Parnaíba
Recife
10°

Plateau of Mato Grosso
Xingu
Brazilian Highlands
São Francisco
Salvador
BRASILIA
Goiânia
Belo Horizonte

4

BOLIVIA
LA PAZ
Lake Titicaca
SUCRE
Potosí
Santa Cruz
Atacama Desierto de

Paraguay
Paraná
Gran Chaco
PARAGUAY
ASUNCIÓN
Iguaçu Falls
Corrientes
São Paulo
Rio de Janeiro

20°

TROPIC OF CAPRICORN

Porto Alegre

5

Aconcagua 6960
Mendoza
Córdoba
Sante Fe
P A M P A S
BUENOS AIRES
A R G E N T I N A
San Miguel de Tucuman
URUGUAY
MONTEVIDEO

30°

Mar del Plata
Colorado
Bahía Blanca

6

A T L A N T I C

Comodoro Rivadavia

40°

O C E A N

7

FALKLAND IS. (UK)
Port Stanley
Magellan's Strait
Punta Arenas
Tierra del Fuego
Cape Horn
South Georgia (UK)

50°

PACIFIC OCEAN
TROPIC OF CAPRICORN

| A | B | C | D | E | F | G |
| 90° | 80° | 70° | 60° | 50° | 40° | 30° | 20° |

8

55

OCEANIA: Countries and Capitals

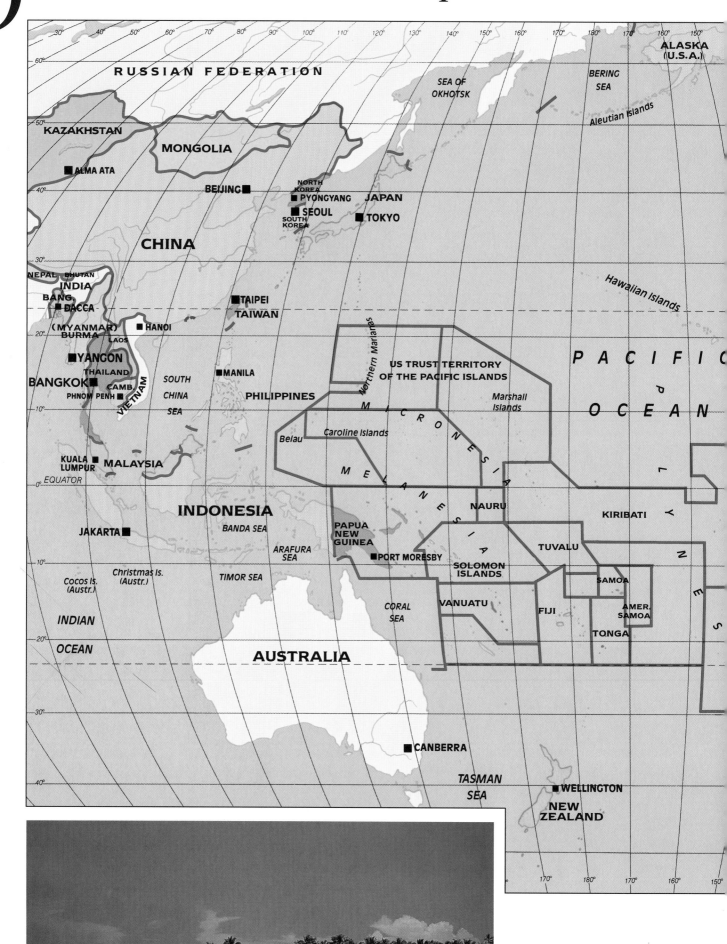

RUSSIAN FEDERATION

ALASKA (U.S.A.)

SEA OF OKHOTSK

BERING SEA

Aleutian Islands

KAZAKHSTAN

■ALMA ATA

MONGOLIA

BEIJING■

NORTH KOREA
■PYONGYANG
■SEOUL
SOUTH KOREA

JAPAN

■TOKYO

CHINA

NEPAL BHUTAN
INDIA
BANG.
■DACCA

■TAIPEI
TAIWAN

Hawaiian Islands

(MYANMAR) BURMA
■HANOI
LAOS

■YANGON
THAILAND
BANGKOK■
CAMB.
PHNOM PENH■ VIETNAM

SOUTH CHINA SEA

■MANILA

PHILIPPINES

Northern Marianas

US TRUST TERRITORY OF THE PACIFIC ISLANDS

Marshall Islands

PACIFIC

MICRONESIA

OCEAN

Belau

Caroline Islands

MELANESIA

KUALA LUMPUR■ MALAYSIA

EQUATOR

INDONESIA

BANDA SEA

NAURU

KIRIBATI

POLYNESIA

JAKARTA■

ARAFURA SEA

PAPUA NEW GUINEA

■PORT MORESBY

SOLOMON ISLANDS

TUVALU

Christmas Is. (Austr.)

TIMOR SEA

VANUATU

SAMOA

Cocos Is. (Austr.)

CORAL SEA

FIJI

AMER. SAMOA

INDIAN

TONGA

OCEAN

AUSTRALIA

■CANBERRA

TASMAN SEA

■WELLINGTON

NEW ZEALAND

Of the thousands of small islands scattered across the Pacific, some are the tips of volcanoes that rise up from the ocean bed; others, like this one in Samoa, are coral atolls, made up of the skeletons of tiny sea creatures.

56

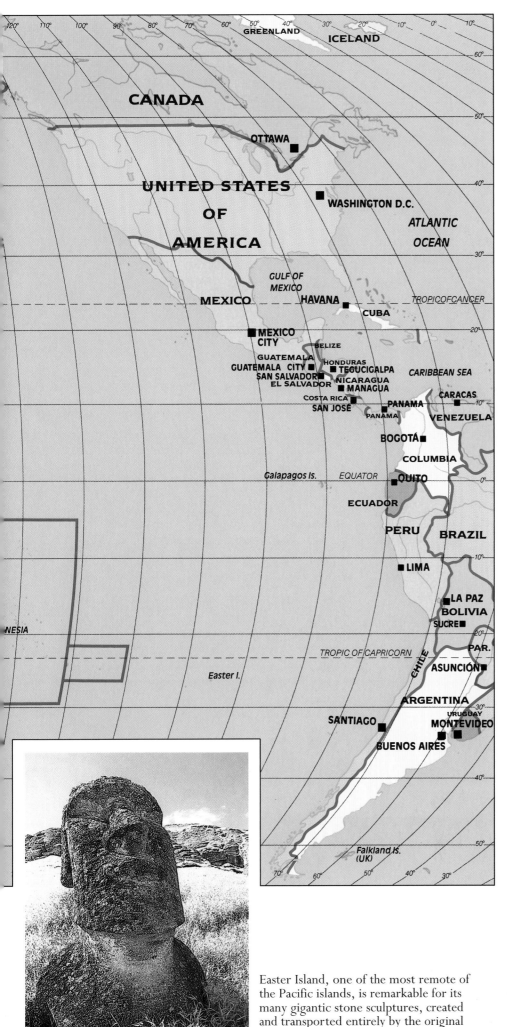

GREENLAND

ICELAND

CANADA

OTTAWA ■

UNITED STATES

OF

AMERICA

■ **WASHINGTON D.C.**

ATLANTIC

OCEAN

GULF OF
MEXICO

MEXICO   **HAVANA** ■

TROPIC OF CANCER

CUBA

■ **MEXICO
CITY**

BELIZE

GUATEMALA
GUATEMALA CITY ■   HONDURAS
SAN SALVADOR ■ ■ **TEGUCIGALPA**
EL SALVADOR ■ **NICARAGUA**
■ **MANAGUA**   **CARIBBEAN SEA**

COSTA RICA ■
SAN JOSÉ   **PANAMA** ■   **CARACAS** ■

PANAMA   **VENEZUELA**

BOGOTÁ ■

COLUMBIA

Galapagos Is.   EQUATOR   ■ **QUITO**

ECUADOR

PERU   **BRAZIL**

■ **LIMA**

■ **LA PAZ**
BOLIVIA
SUCRE ■

NESIA

TROPIC OF CAPRICORN   **PAR.**

Easter I.   **ASUNCIÓN** ■

ARGENTINA
URUGUAY
SANTIAGO ■   **MONTEVIDEO**
■ ■
BUENOS AIRES

Falkland Is.
(UK)

Easter Island, one of the most remote of
the Pacific islands, is remarkable for its
many gigantic stone sculptures, created
and transported entirely by the original
Aborigine inhabitants.

Oceania comprises tens of thousands of islands scattered over the largest and deepest ocean in the world, the Pacific Ocean, and sometimes includes Australia and New Zealand. The vast area of the Pacific stretches from Australia to Easter Island, and from Hawaii to New Zealand. Only about 3000 of the islands are large enough to have names. The three main groups are Polynesia, Melanesia and Micronesia.

Polynesia, the largest group, lies in the centre of the Pacific. Most of its islands are volcanic and have risen from the floor of the Pacific Ocean, where two plates of the earth's crust have collided. Many of the islands are subject to volcanic eruptions and earthquakes. The best-known islands in Polynesia are Tahiti, Tonga, Samoa and Hawaii. Polynesians are tall, handsome, golden-skinned people.

Melanesia is an arc of islands that spreads southeast from New Guinea. This group includes islands such as the Solomon Islands, Vanuatu and Fiji. The Melanesians are dark-skinned with frizzy hair. They live in small village units, each of which may have its own language .

Micronesia is an arc of small coral islands, which includes the Marianas, Caroline Islands, Kiribati, Nauru and Guam. Most of the islands lie on or north of the Equator. Micronesians have copper-coloured skin and straight black hair. In the small islands, tourism and the production of copra are the main economic activities. Some resources are found on the larger islands. Fiji supplies timber to Australia and New Zealand, and sugar to Britain. New Caledonia has deposits of nickel, and Nauru produces phosphates for fertilisers. The great distance of the islands from major markets restricts any important development, and most of the people survive by subsistence farming.

57

AUSTRALIA

Australia is the world's smallest continental landmass. It is a huge, sparsely populated island state in the southern hemisphere. The country is divided up into the seven self-governing states of New South Wales, Northern Territory, Queensland, South Australia, Tasmania, Victoria, and Western Australia. The capital, Canberra, is situated in the Australian Capital Territory. Most of the population live in or near the east coast, mainly in the cities of Sydney, Melbourne and Brisbane.

The Aborigines were the first inhabitants of Australia. They arrived about 40,000 years ago and were nomadic hunters. Europeans started to settle in Australia about 200 years ago, after Captain Cook discovered the fertile east coast. The first settlement was a convict colony at Botany Bay. Gradually, as more people arrived, mainly from Britain, crops such as wheat and fruit were grown and sheep and cattle raised.

In the 19th century gold was discovered, and the population increased dramatically. Prospectors arrived hoping to strike gold and become rich. Settlements known as Gold Towns, such as Bendigo and Coolgardie, sprang up overnight. The Gold Rush did not last but people continued to settle in

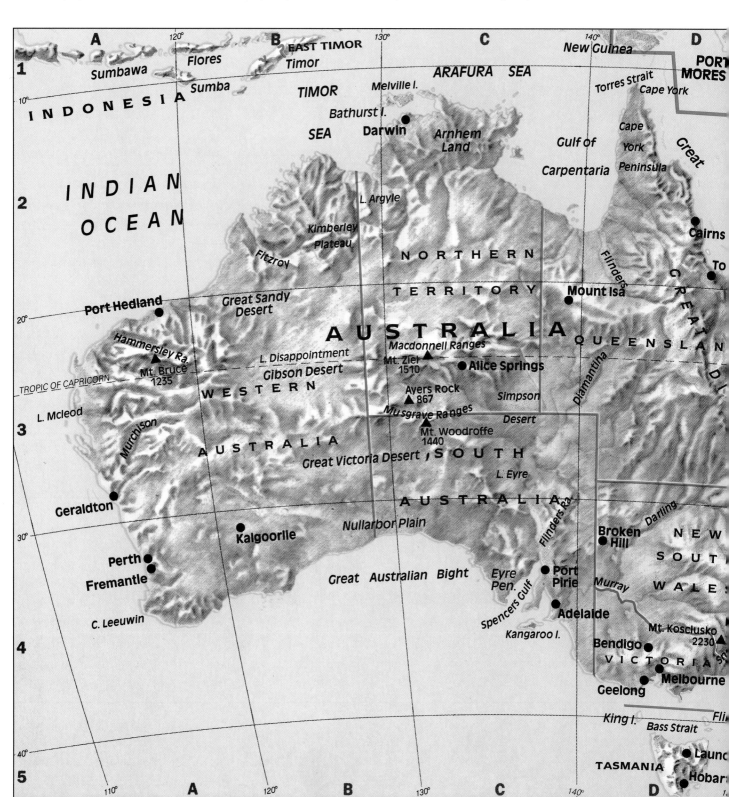

Australia. Since 1945 the population has doubled.

Australia can be divided physically into three main parts—the high ground and plateau in the west, the interior lowlands in the middle, and the mountain ranges in the east. Much of the country is very dry, and in the central and western regions there are large areas of desert. Only in the east is the climate suitable for growing wheat, oats and fruit, and for the huge sheep farms that make Australia the world's largest wool producer. In Queensland, where the climate is hot and wet, sugar cane can be grown in the lowlands.

Tasmania produces apples and timber, and all states produce wine. The best known vine-growing regions are the Hunter Valley in New South Wales and the Barossa Valley in South Australia.

Huge quantities of easily mined coal is Australia's main export. Hydroelectric power from the Snowy Mountains and reserves of oil and natural gas make the country self-sufficient in electricity. Mineral deposits are rich, and Australia is a leading producer of iron ore, copper, lead, zinc, manganese, nickel, uranium, tin and bauxite. Precious metals such as silver, gold and platinum are also produced .

One of the most famous tourist attractions in Australia is the Great Barrier Reef. This is the largest coral reef system in the world. It stretches for over 2000 kilometres in the Coral Sea along the coast of Queensland. The reef, which is up to 500 metres thick, extends up to 300 kilometres from land in the south. The waters around it are dotted with hundreds of islands.

Sydney Harbour has acquired a new landmark in the sails of Sydney Opera House. Australia's largest city and main port lies on the east coast of the country near Botany Bay, where the first European settlement (a prison colony) was established in 1778.

Many of these have become tourist resorts or bases for underwater swimmers who come to explore the reef.

Another striking feature of the landscape in central Australia is Ayers Rock. This is a huge monolith in the Northern Territory near Alice Springs. It rises to 348 metres above the plain and is more than eight kilometres around the base. The Rock is an Aboriginal sacred site, and many beautiful paintings and carvings can be seen in caves within it. It stands in a national park, and more than 50,000 people visit it each year.

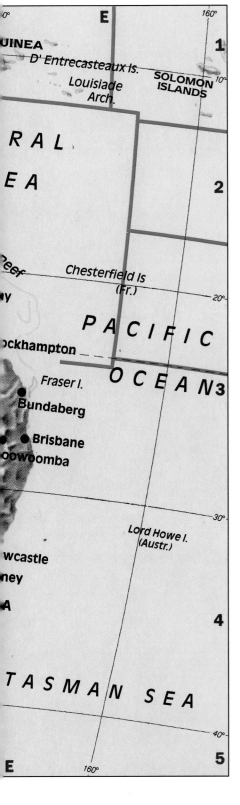

Ayers Rock is a majestic outcrop of granite in the centre of Australia's arid outback (interior). It is an Aboriginal holy place and has many beautiful rock carvings.

NEW ZEALAND and the SOUTH PACIFIC ISLANDS

New Zealand lies southeast of Australia in the South Pacific Ocean. It consists of two major islands, North Island and South Island, and several small islands, including Stewart Island and the Chatham Islands.

The first people to settle in New Zealand, around AD900, were the Maoris. They reached New Zealand by sailing from the Polynesian Islands in the Pacific. In 1840 it became a British colony, and many people emigrated from Europe to New Zealand. In 1907 it declared independence. The capital, Wellington, is situated on North Island. Today the population is a mixture of Maoris and people of mainly British descent.

Most of the population live in North Island, where the climate is warm and tropical. It has fertile grazing land highly favourable for raising dairy cattle and sheep. Cheese, butter and meat are important agricultural exports. North Island has many active volcanoes, such as Mount Egmont on the west coast. Around Rotorua, hot water bubbles out of the ground, and in some places the pressure is so great that geysers force water 70 metres into the air. The steam from these can be used to drive electric power stations.

South Island is mountainous and fringed on the east coast by extensive plains, where cereals are grown and huge flocks of sheep are grazed. The snow-capped peaks of the Southern Alps run the whole length of the island. The mountains rise dramatically from the plains, and 20 of the peaks exceed 3000 metres. The highest is Mount Cook (3765 metres). In the highest regions there are ice fields and glaciers.

Farming and farming-related industries are the basis of New Zealand's wealth. Farms are well managed, and livestock produce very high yields of wool, meat and milk. As the population is small, there are great surpluses of agricultural products, and a high proportion is exported. It is the world's leading exporter of lamb and dairy products. The timber industry is now being developed, and additional land has been planted with vines in order to expand the wine industry.

Auckland is the largest city in New Zealand. It is situated on North Island and is spread over many extinct volcanoes. It was formerly the capital city and is the chief port and industrial centre.

In the region around Rotorua, on North Island, hot water bubbles out of the ground. In some places. the underground pressure is such that tall geysers of water and steam are forced out.

New Zealand is the world's largest exporter of lamb, and has many huge sheep farms especially on South Island.

Milford Sound, in the extreme southwest of South Island, is one of the several spectacular sea inlets that has earned the area the name of Fiordland, after similar coastal features in Norway.

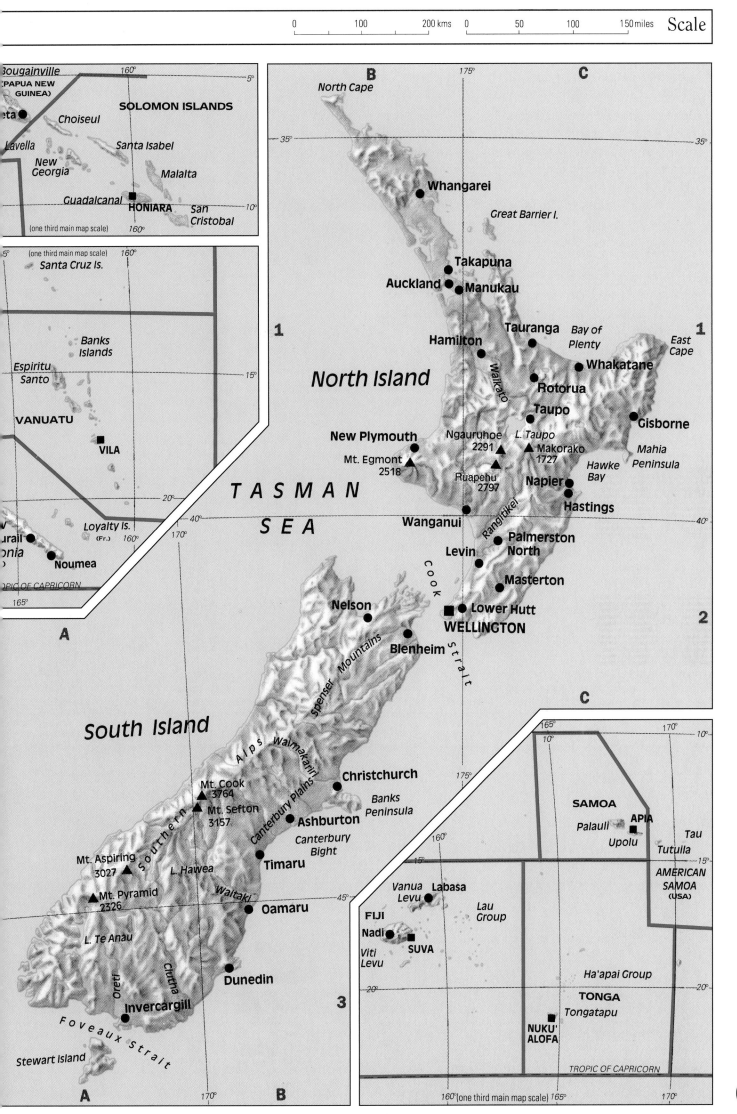

Scale

0   100   200 kms   0   50   100   150 miles

SOLOMON ISLANDS

Bougainville
(PAPUA NEW
GUINEA)
eta
Lavella
Choiseul
New
Georgia
Santa Isabel
Malaita
Guadalcanal
HONIARA
San
Cristobal

(one third main map scale)

(one third main map scale)
Santa Cruz Is.

Banks
Islands
Espiritu
Santo
VANUATU
VILA
Loyalty Is.
(Fr.)
urail
onia
Noumea
TROPIC OF CAPRICORN

North Cape

Whangarei

Great Barrier I.

Takapuna
Auckland   **Manukau**

Tauranga
Hamilton   Bay of
Plenty   East
Cape
North Island   Waikato   **Whakatane**
Rotorua
Taupo   Gisborne
New Plymouth   Ngauruhoe
2291   L. Taupo   Makorako
1727
Mt. Egmont
2518   Ruapehu
2797   Mahia
Peninsula
Hawke
Bay
Napier
Hastings
Wanganui   Rangitikei
**Palmerston
North**
Levin
Masterton

**T A S M A N
S E A**

Nelson
Cook
Blenheim   Strait
Lower Hutt
WELLINGTON

Spenser Mountains

South Island

Alps   Waimakariri
Southern
Mt. Cook
3764
Mt. Sefton
3157   **Christchurch**
Canterbury Plains   Banks
Peninsula
Ashburton
Canterbury
Bight
Mt. Aspiring
3027   L. Hawea
Waitaki   **Timaru**
Mt. Pyramid
2326   Oreti   Clutha
Waitaki   **Oamaru**
L. Te Anau

Dunedin
Invercargill
Foveaux Strait
Stewart Island

SAMOA
Palauli   **APIA**
Upolu   Tau
Tutuila
**AMERICAN
SAMOA**
(USA)
Vanua
Levu   **Labasa**
Lau
Group
FIJI
Nadi
Viti
Levu   **SUVA**

Ha'apai Group

TONGA
**NUKU'
ALOFA**   Tongatapu

TROPIC OF CAPRICORN

(one third main map scale)

61

POLAR REGIONS

The polar regions of the world are the areas inside the Arctic and Antarctic Circles, the imaginary lines around the North and South Poles of the Earth.

The Arctic is a region of relatively shallow sea almost completely surrounded by the landmasses of Asia, Europe and North America. It is so cold that the sea around the North Pole is permanently frozen in winter to a depth of three metres.

The land around the Arctic Circle is called tundra. It is covered in snow and ice during the winter, but in the short summer the surface snow melts and small patches of mosses and lichens are able to grow. In the middle of winter there are days when the sun never rises and in midsummer when it never sets.

The only people who live permanently in the Arctic are Eskimos, or Inuit. They live by hunting, fishing and trapping. In northern Scandinavia the Lapps live by herding reindeer.

Most of the island of Greenland lies within the Arctic Circle. Eskimos have lived here since 2500BC, and Vikings settled there in AD986. Greenland is now a self-governing province of Denmark.

Eskimos in Greenland and the Arctic regions of Canada fish, often through holes in the ice, and hunt seals and whales.

Antarctica is a huge continent surrounding the South Pole and is entirely covered by nearly three kilometres of ice. It has the coldest and harshest climate in the world. The lowest recorded temperature of -89.2° Celsius was taken at Vostok Station in 1983. In the winter, fierce winds blow and it is very dry. There are between four and five months of continuous daylight in summer and four to five months of darkness in winter. In the summer months, pieces of ice break off from the edge of the ice sheet to form icebergs.

Animals living in Antarctica include penguins and seals, and they depend on the sea for their food supply. There are no permanent inhabitants in Antarctica, but there are a number of manned research camps and weather stations operated by several countries, including the U.K.

It is thought that reserves of oil and valuable minerals may lie beneath the ice, but so far a method of extracting them has not been discovered.

Huge colonies of penguins inhabit Antarctica, especially near the coast, where they are able to survive the harsh conditions by feeding on fish.

The base on King George Island operated by Chile is one of many scientific research stations on Antarctica. These are the only human settlements on this inhospitable continent.

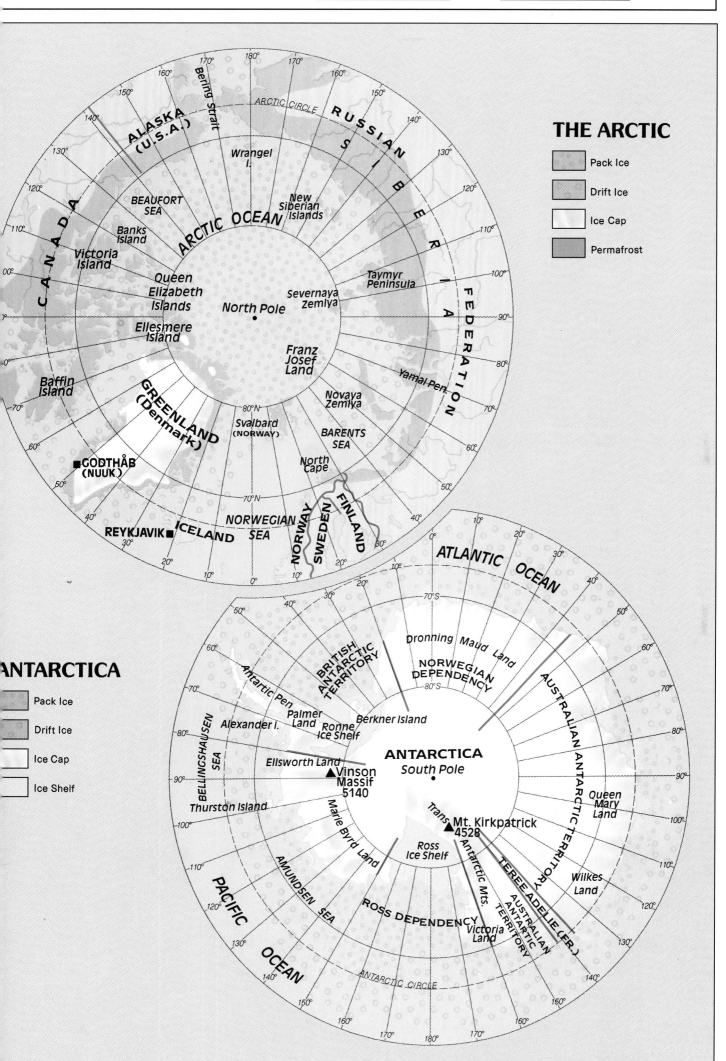

Scale

0 400 800 1200 1600 Km   0 200 400 600 800 1000 Miles

THE ARCTIC

- Pack Ice
- Drift Ice
- Ice Cap
- Permafrost

ALASKA (U.S.A.)

ARCTIC CIRCLE

R U S S I A N

170° 180° 170° 160° 150° 140° 130°

Bering Strait

Wrangel I.

BEAUFORT SEA

New Siberian Islands

Banks Island

ARCTIC OCEAN

C A N A D A

Victoria Island

S I B E R I A

Queen Elizabeth Islands

Taymyr Peninsula

Severnaya Zemlya

North Pole

F E D E R A T I O N

Ellesmere Island

Franz Josef Land

Yamal Pen.

Baffin Island

GREENLAND (Denmark)

80°N

Novaya Zemlya

Svalbard (NORWAY)

BARENTS SEA

■GODTHÅB (NUUK)

North Cape

70°N

NORWEGIAN SEA

REYKJAVIK■ ICELAND

NORWAY SWEDEN FINLAND

ANTARCTICA

- Pack Ice
- Drift Ice
- Ice Cap
- Ice Shelf

ATLANTIC OCEAN

Dronning Maud Land

NORWEGIAN DEPENDENCY

BRITISH ANTARCTIC TERRITORY

80°S

Antarctic Pen.

AUSTRALIAN ANTARCTIC TERRITORY

Palmer Land

Berkner Island

Alexander I.

BELLINGSHAUSEN SEA

Ronne Ice Shelf

Ellsworth Land

ANTARCTICA
South Pole

Queen Mary Land

▲ Vinson Massif 5140

Thurston Island

Marie Byrd Land

Trans

▲ Mt. Kirkpatrick 4528

Ross Ice Shelf

Wilkes Land

PACIFIC OCEAN

AMUNDSEN SEA

ROSS DEPENDENCY

Antarctic Mts.

TERRE ADÉLIE (FR.)

AUSTRALIAN ANTARCTIC TERRITORY

Victoria Land

ANTARCTIC CIRCLE

63

QUICK INDEX